BOKKEN
Art of the Japanese Sword

by Dave Lowry

Editor: Mike Lee
Graphic Design: Karen Massad

Art Production: Junko Sadjadpour
Ludovic Szvercsak

© 1986 Ohara Publications, Inc.
All rights reserved
Printed in the United States of America
Library of Congress Catalog Card Number: 85-63391
ISBN 0-89750-104-7
Thirth-sixth printing 2004

BLACK BELT BOOKS
A Division of **OHARA 🅟 PUBLICATIONS, INC.**
World Leader in Martial Arts Publications

WARNING

*The sword was to be far more
than a simple weapon; it had to be an
answer to life's questions.*
    —**Musashi,** *by Eiji Yoshikawa*

Acknowledgement

A sincere note of appreciation is due Haruo Matsuoka, of
Hombu Aikido, who was somewhat askance at the
unexpected appearance of a Yagyu *kenshi* with blue eyes, but
who nonetheless performed as my assistant for the *kumitachi*
sequences with considerable expertise.

About the Author

Dave Lowry is an author and a swordsman of the 21st generation of the Yagyu Shinkage tradition. Of the classical Japanese martial schools, the Yagyu is one of the most venerated, with a close connection to Zen and the politics of feudal Japan. Dave Lowry began his training in the classical art of Japanese swordsmanship in 1968 under the tutelage of Ryokichi Kotaro of Nara Prefecture. Lowry's training in these ancient arts has descended in an unbroken line that began with Yagyu Muneyoshi in the 16th century. His *ryu-ha keizu* (martial arts school genealogy) includes several warriors of note: Yagyu Toshiyori, first headmaster of Owari Yagyu Shinkage-ryu; Matsunaga Keinosuke, who participated in the battle at Sekigahara as a retainer of the Lord Miyoshi; Osada Itaro, teacher of fencing and tea ceremony to the sixth shogun, Tokugawa Yoshimune; and Okimoto Shuzo, retainer and assistant to the *fudai* (principal lord), Matsudaira Keiei.

Lowry's martial arts experience also includes training in Kodokan judo and karate-do. He currently lives and trains near St. Louis, Missouri.

Introduction

In the past few years, there has been an exceptional interest shown in the various cultural facets of traditional Japan. Classes in such diverse Japanese Ways as *chado* (the art of the tea ceremony), and *naginata-do* (the art of the samurai's halberd) have sprung up in different places in the Occident, to join more popular Ways already there, such as *judo, kendo,* and *kado* (the art of *ikebana,* or flower arrangement). There are, in fact, groups of Westerners now devoted to such esoteric forms as *kodo,* the art of incense appreciation, and *Noh,* the oldest form of Japanese theater. This interest has been particularly gratifying to note, since in many cases those involved are not just learning the mere surface techniques or skills of these arts, but are seeking an in-depth understanding of their principles and philosophical and historical meanings.

The interest has affected Western martial artists as well, a number of whom, despite years of experience in the budo, seem to have only recently discovered that these martial Ways are a part of the warp and weave of Japan's feudal past and that, by extension, those who pursue them have a dependence upon this past, and a significant stake in its continuation. Like others engaged in the study of various Ways and arts, these budoka have undertaken a search for their "roots" in the martial Ways of old Japan, in an effort to understand better where it is they and their arts have come from.

Unfortunately, this is no simple proposition. Many of the classical *ryu* that are the fountainheads of the modern budo are extinct, and those that have survived are virtually closed to all but a handful of practitioners who have the time, social connections, financial resources, and not unimportantly, fluency in Japanese, to gain admittance. It has become common in the past two decades, to find non-Japanese studying in the dojo of *iaido* (sword drawing) and *kyudo* (archery) masters, and some have even penetrated to the area of the older *bujutsu*, the classical arts of the samurai. Even for the most serious and dedicated budoka, however, the chances of training in a budo-ryu are slim. Nearly all writing and research in the historical and philosophical foundations of the budo are in Japanese, and even at that, they are only words, dates, and genealogies for the most part, with nothing but a hint of the soul and spirit of the arts.

Yet despite these bleak prospects, all is not lost for the budoka who wishes to delve into the origins of his martial discipline. Various connections remain. Certainly one of the most fascinating and rewarding lies in the techniques of *suburi* (exercises performed in the manner of traditional Japanese fencing), with the wooden sword, or *bokken*. True, the student of suburi uses this practice weapon instead of a live sword (*katana*) and the movements are not so clearly lethal as those of the feudal warrior's art, but with his bokken, the modern budoka may train on two important levels. On one, he builds the physical stamina, rhythms, and adroit body movements of traditional swordsmanship. On the other, he achieves something of the animating spirit of the traditional swordsman. He is, through the refinement of his practice, linked in a very real way to his past, for it is from the principles of swordsmanship that the budo of today have based their teachings, no matter what their present form.

I have been fortunate in my years of following in the path of the martial arts and Ways of Japan, to experience the dual sides of that link, with exposure to training in both the classical art of the sword, and in the modern disciplines of judo and karate-do. Like many practitioners of either, I have grave concerns for their future. The bujutsu, or arts of the samurai, are quite fragile, like vintage wines that cannot travel well or survive a great deal of change. They remain extant largely because of a select group of devoted adherents, mostly in Japan, who are making every effort to retain their original flavor. The modern budo are a bit more sturdy in comparison, since their founders encouraged their study by larger groups of individuals. In fact, those founders went to special effort to introduce the budo to the world outside Japan. They have succeeded. Today, the practitioners of judo, karate-do, aikido, kendo, and so on, number into the hundreds of thousands.

This popularity is healthy but with such an emphasis on quantity, the quality of earlier eras is in risk of being compromised. Already some of the budo forms have perverted their purpose to accomodate sport and competition. Others have had their names or surface appearances unscrupulously stolen by thieves who use them to disguise their inferior teaching and practice.

And so, in the final analysis, both the old and new martial arts and Ways face serious threats. There is little we can do, no "Save the Budo/Bujutsu Fund" to send a check to. No efforts at conservation will insure a renewed supply of the stuff.

The only aid the individual can bring to the budo he follows is to set aside his personal predilections and desires, and attempt to pursue it with a pure heart, staying as closely as possible to the course set by those who've gone before him. Through study, through interaction with his seniors, teachers and masters, and of course, through incessant and selfless training, he must make the effort to comprehend the true meaning of the budo, and to follow it unswervingly.

However, there is one more thing the budoka might do, regardless of his particular budo, to further his understanding of it. He might take up the bokken, and learn to handle it proficiently. This may seem like a rather strange way of deepening one's grasp of some of the budo, especially forms like judo or karate-do, which are basically empty handed. But no matter what the specific nature of the budo, each of them had their inception in the age of the warrior, and in *bushido,* his code of behavior. All the martial Ways share this obligation to the samurai. Therefore, to take up the weapon he considered central to his life, or at least a facsimile of it, is to take the first step in realizing what his life was all about. It is to forge more tightly that link between the 20th-century budoka and his predecessor, in a visible, tangible way. The student who trains with the bokken cannot help but take a greater interest in the way of the warrior, as he learns the technical aspects of cutting with the sword and learning to mold its actions with those of his own body. And in a philosophical and physical sense, he returns to his roots, growing stronger in the process. These are the benefits of training in suburi, the basic techniques of the bokken.

As we face the next century, we should pause and look back, to see where we've come from, in order to gain a wider perspective on where we're going. This is the fundamental rationale for taking up the sword today.

I would encourage every budoka, or anyone else with an interest in old Japan, to make suburi training a daily part of his or her life. It is my hope that this modest volume will serve as a beginning guide for those who do.

—D.L.

Contents

The Way of the Sword and the Way of
Zen are identical, for they have the
same purpose—that of killing the ego.
—Yamada Jirokichi, of Jikishinkage-ryu

ORIGINS
OF THE BOKKEN

The history of the Japanese sword and of swordsmanship in that country is so ancient that no one could hope
to discover its sources. Records of the sword in combat
are found in both the *Nihon Shoki* and the *Kojiki,* two annals of the mythic
Shindai, or "Period of the Gods," which preceded written history in Japan.
In these earliest centuries, swords were copied after those made in China,
long straight sabers, used mainly for thrusting. Later, as warfare developed
into more of a science, the Japanese warrior began to carry a slightly shorter
sword, with a pronounced curve in the blade and a two-handed grip. This

tachi was most effective when swung from atop a horse in battle, where its length and curvature allowed wide, swinging slashes.

The use of the bokken in swordsmanship was an addition to the art that did not come along until Muromachi Period (1336-1600), when the emphasis on the sword shifted from battlefield tactics to a more individualized dueling. This form of single combat was a specialty of the *ryu*, the organized systems of teaching martial arts which sprung up during the period, after a century-long age of civil strife that saw the emergence and subsequent dominance of the professional fighting man of Japan, the samurai. Greatly increased, too, was the status of his military arts in general, and of his swordsmanship in particular.

Previously, exponents of the craft of fencing had little in the way of instruction available to them. Expertise was gained through experience; those who were slow learners rarely were around long enough to regret their mistakes. But as better swords were forged, as one-on-one dueling (on and off the battlefield) replaced the charging, cavalry style swinging of the weapon, the techniques of fencing progressed rapidly. Under the auspices of the ryu, methods were broken down and analyzed, evaluated as to their effectiveness, and taught in an orderly, prescribed manner according to a set curriculum. Each of the many ryu had differing ways of accomplishing this, but they all had one need in common. All of them had to have some means by which aspiring swordsmen could practice the techniques of fencing with a modicum of safety. The answer to their problem was the bokken.

No doubt some form of wooden mock sword existed earlier in Japanese history, but it was with the birth of the ryu system that craftsmen began to fashion the bokken still in existence today, little changed. The bokken offered several advantages over a live blade in training at the ryu dojo. Aside from the obvious safety factor it afforded trainees, it was also a good way to preserve the edges of expensive steel swords. The Japanese *katana* is forged so that its spine is quite malleable, allowing it to absorb considerable punishment in striking and thrusting, yet it has a brittle, razor-sharp edge that permits its great cutting power. From this combination of hard and soft emerged a deadly bladed weapon, but one that could easily be damaged if the cutting surface came in harsh contact with another hard object. Frequently, katana were nicked and even broken in combat. Therefore, rather than risk flawing an expensive blade, the use of the bokken permitted the novice fencer to make contact with an opponent's weapon in the training hall, without serious damage to the sword.

By the middle of the 16th century, there were over 900 ryu in Japan devoted to *kenjutsu,* the art of the sword, and the bokken was the central training weapon of virtually all of them. And, as kenjutsu grew ever more refined, the improvement was reflected in a more sophisticated employment of the bokken. It was only a matter of time before some enterprising swordsmen discovered that the bokken had not only an important place in training, but a more practical value as well, as a formidable weapon in its own right.

Historical tales of swordslingers and their art, called *kenshi kodan*, are full of examples of master *kenshi* who met opponents armed with live, steel weapons, with nothing but a bokken in their hands. Upon hearing such stories, the listener's likely to be filled with admiration for a warrior so bold. Actually, however, for the master, the difference between the bokken and the *shinken* (live sword) was minimal. In fact, some fencers insisted the wooden weapon was superior, particularly in one vital way. To understand why they felt that way, it's necessary to know that the Japanese sword consists of a long blade with a tang that is fitted into a wooden handle and fixed there by means of one or two small pins slotted through handle and tang. This makes the katana secure, but due to the nature of the comparatively thin steel blade and the hollow handle, a certain amount of torqueing can occur, especially when the sword is swung hard in one direction, then twisted and quickly reversed back in the opposite way, a movement common to many ryu, called *kesa gake*. Kesa gake places a tremendous stress on the blade and handle connection, so much so that the movement can actually snap one or both, breaking the weapon at a most crucial time. Then too, Japan's climate is notoriously damp, and even with the best of care, it was all too easy for a wooden handle to succumb to various forms of rot, weakening the katana invisibly from within. Neither of these potential defects were to be found in the solid, one piece bokken.

It should not be believed that the bokken replaced the shinken as the swordsman's favorite tool in fighting, but as a number of famous stories illustrate, it was often used with extreme success in matters of life and death.

Perhaps the best-known encounter involving a wooden sword was that of Miyamoto Musashi's, who met and defeated Sasaki Kojiro on a sandy islet in the middle of the Kanmon Straits, in southern Japan.

Musashi, of course, is famed as the archetypal swordslinger-artist-philosopher so beloved in Japanese history and folktale. He was born in Harima Province, a member of the Shinmen clan. Early in his life, he adopted his mother's clan name, becoming known thereafter as Musashi Miyamoto. Although both sides of his family were of samurai rank, and his father is even reputed to have founded his own ryu, Musashi could not claim to have trained in any of the classical styles of his day. Instead, his approach to swordsmanship was to learn by doing, and considering the 70-some victories he is credited with during his lifetime, his approach must have been a good one.

Sasaki Kojiro supposedly came from Jokyoji, in old Echizen Province. According to tales told about him, he joined the Tomita-ryu as a young child, after being adopted by Tomita Seigen himself, the headmaster and founder of the ryu. After mastering the techniques of the Tomita style of fencing, he won a number of duels, including one against his uncle, and in time he created his own style of swordplay, the Ganryu. Sasaki's skill with the sword was said to be almost superhuman. He was famed for his ability at *tsubame-gaeshi,* a stroke that brought the katana up and down in one slashing motion that was so swift it resembled the whirling flight of a swallow.

Both Musashi and Sasaki were guests of the daimyo of the Hosokawa clan, of Kokura, at the time of their duel. Since Kokura is on the coast of the island of Kyushu, it was decided that their match would take place on a small sandbar in the middle of the sea channel separating Kyushu from Honshu, the main island of Japan. Clan officials banned spectators from the island on the day of the duel, but it was crowded with them anyway, most of them certain the young, unknown swordsman Musashi would be easily killed by Sasaki. At the hour of the Dragon (8:00 a.m.), the agreed-upon time for their match, Sasaki was ferried out to the island. He checked his sword fittings one last time, surveyed the crowd, and then gazed quietly out into the channel, where his opponent would appear.

Yet the minutes passed, and became hours, and still there was no sign of Musashi. On the day of his greatest challenge, the iconoclastic warrior was oversleeping at an inn near the beach on Kyushu. He was finally awakened by the innkeeper and hustled down to the shore to be rowed to his appointment. While the boat rocked in the swells of the Kammon Straits, Musashi sat sleepily in the prow. Apparently to wake himself, he took up a knife and a spare oar and began carving, producing by the time he'd reached the island, a crude sort of bokken from his labor. It was this weapon that he clutched, leaping ashore to face Sasaki.

Sasaki, irritated, chided Musashi for being late, and laughed scornfully at his freshly carved "sword." He drew his own weapon, a fine blade nicknamed "Frost Silver," and then threw its scabbard into the waves to indicate his willingness to fight to the death.

"You must have little confidence in yourself, throwing away a good scabbard as if you'll never need it again," Musashi observed, a remark intended to unbalance Sasaki's mental poise. Then he gripped his wooden weapon tightly and pointed it at Sasaki's throat. The fight had begun.

The two men advanced towards one another, each feeling out with every step the other's posture and strategy. A single error, the blink of an eye or a foot slipping even fractionally in the sand, would have meant disaster. Time slowed, then stopped, then was frozen, as Sasaki leaped at Musashi, striking with vicious intent, using his notorious tsubame gaeshi strike. At the same instant, Musashi jumped forward, bringing his wooden sword down with a terrible shout. For a long moment after their simultaneous clash, what had happened wasn't at all clear to the spectators. A gust of wind caught at the headband on Musashi's forehead, pulling it away, and with a gasp, the onlookers saw that it had been sliced by Sasaki's sword. Surely Musashi's skull had been split open by the weapon's stroke. But in another second, the outcome of the battle was obvious. The audience saw that Musashi had so carefully timed his jump that he'd come within a hairsbreadth of Sasaki's katana, so close it cut his headband, yet he was the one who delivered the fatal strike, with his bokken. Sasaki collapsed, his head crushed.

The folktale of Musashi and Sasaki Kojiro is a famous one; few martial artists have not heard or read or seen at least a half dozen versions of it. It does not seem to matter much that the whole event might never have happened at all, or that the figure of Sasaki Kojiro has never even been historically ascertained. It's a dramatic, exciting story, treasured by those with an interest in the martial arts of old Japan. More importantly, however, from the budoka's perspective, it's an illustration of how highly the wooden sword was viewed as a weapon of real combat.

Even if the story of Musashi's victory over Sasaki is nothing more than that, it's evidence of the bokken's place in the feudal warrior's arsenal, and in fact, other stories, of historical provenance, relate the use of the bokken in duels. A good example is provided by the match between Itto Ittosai Kagehisa, founder of the Itto (one sword) -ryu, and Migogami Tenzen. Although Tenzen wielded a sharp steel sword, Ittosai beat him decisively with a bokken—some accounts maintain it wasn't even that, but merely a piece of kindling he picked up from a woodpile—showing such perfect control over the weapon that he defeated his challenger without hurting him. Tenzen became a student of Ittosai's. Many years later, after changing his name to Ono Taadaki, he became the second headmaster of his master's Itto-ryu.

As long as kenjutsu flourished during the feudal era, the use of the bokken in training and combat continued to be improved and studied earnestly. However, with the fall of the Tokugawa Dynasty and the abolishment of feudalism in Japan in 1867, the martial arts of the samurai fell into decline. Swordsmanship in particular, was drastically altered. Emphasis was shifted, as kenjutsu evolved into kendo, to character development and sporting competition. Kendo replaced the bokken with the *shinai*, a flexible weapon of lengths of bamboo lashed together. The shinai was an even safer alternative to the real katana than the bokken but, unlike the solid wooden sword, the bamboo substitute had no curvature, a different balance, and a weight far less than the real thing. It allowed kendo practitioners to strike with a snappy speed that encouraged *hitting* rather than *cutting.*

While the employment of the shinai greatly increased kendo's popularity, it eclipsed the more realistic practicalities of classical swordsmanship. The art's original principles were dependent upon a few isolated ryu and swordsmen who kept them alive. One who found himself drawn to these principles was Morihei Uyeshiba.

Uyeshiba was born in 1883, in Tanabe, Wakayama Prefecture, the son and descendant of farmers from that rural region. During childhood, Uyeshiba was sickly, but under the guidance of his samurai grandfather, he became strong and robust, training hard in *sumo* and *jujutsu*. Through his early adult years, he traveled extensively in Japan, living in Tokyo, the frontier island of Hokkaido, and even visiting mainland China as an infantryman in the Sino-Japanese War. In each of these places, he continued his study of martial arts. He trained in various styles of jujutsu, as well as in the fencing techniques of the Shinkage-ryu. Later on. Uyeshiba also gained expertise in the arts of the spear and staff, and in the fencing style of the Yagyu-ryu. As his mastery of these disciplines broadened, he grew to understand that, while they may have used different weapons or techniques, at their center, all of them were essentially alike. He reasoned that the swordsman's cut was the same, in terms of the muscles used, placement of the hips, and so on, as striking with the "sword edge" of the empty hand. A pivoting action to avoid an enemy's spear could, by catching the arm or sleeve, be turned into an effective throw using the same force and technique of the pivot. This principle Uyeshiba knew as *riai; ri* meaning "principle," *ai*, a "meeting" or "joining together."

Uyeshiba's theory of riai coincided with the rise of the budo and he eventually founded his own, calling it *aikido*. At the heart of his aikido was riai, and Uyeshiba insisted that those who trained with him learn to manipulate the sword as well as to master the empty-handed techniques of his art.

Modern aikido students continue to follow Uyeshiba's principles, training with the bokken daily to increase their understanding of the art. They have, in fact, become the major proponents of suburi practice with the bokken. But they are not the only budoka who engage in it. Advanced judo students must be familiar with the *goshin-jutsu* kata, which calls for an unarmed defender to disarm an attacker striking with a bokken, and these judoka must train vigorously with the wooden sword to make their mastery of the kata complete. Although kendo still prefers the use of the shinai in competition, recently more and more interest is being shown in kendo dojo for returning to substantial training with the bokken. It is felt by many of the masters of the art, that kendo has become too far removed from kenjutsu, losing not only the spiritual qualities of its predecessor, but much of the physical abilities granted by suburi practice, as well. It is now once more common to see the bokken during kendo sessions, used in conjunction with the shinai to produce better kendo competitors. Even in karate, the bokken plays a useful role, swung in various swings and strikes to develop the arm, shoulder, and trunk muscles so necessary for making good karate strikes, punches, and blocks. An all-Japan karate champion, Takeshi Oishi, who is now an instructor in the Japan Karate Association, credited suburi, performed hundreds of times daily, with increasing his speed and rhythm in competition.

Today, the bokken is found in many budo dojo, recognized by martial artists as a useful tool in mastering the principles of riai conceived by Morihei Uyeshiba long ago. These budoka understand that, whether making a block and kick, or a throw, or a strike with the shinai, the principles of each are the same. And their fundamentals are to be found in suburi, the movements of the wooden sword.

*For years I forged my spirit through the
study of swordsmanship, confronting
every challenge steadfastly. The walls
surrounding me suddenly crumbled. Like
pure dew reflecting the world in crystal
clarity, total awakening has now come.*
  —Yamaoka Tesshu, of Muto-ryu

TRAINING
WITH THE BOKKEN

A great many of those who are drawn to learning to use
the bokken, martial artists or not, approach it with one
of two preconceptions. Since both these are *mis*concep-
tions, before detailing the fundamentals of what suburi practice with the
bokken *is,* it is worthwhile to insert a caveat as to what it is not.

Initially, it's natural to assume—or to hope—that the techniques of
striking and moving with the bokken will resemble the feats of cinematic
swordplay featured in *chambara* (samurai epic motion pictures) which have
enjoyed popularity for years in Japan and which are now being shown in the

West. In these movies, the actors generate dazzling displays of skill, often taking on a score or more attackers, cutting them down with balletic aplomb.

These movies are entertaining, and even those which are purely fictional can offer fascinating glimpses into feudal Japanese history. Then too, many times the actors in them are indeed students of the sword. The most familiar of these to Western audiences is Toshiro Mifune, who has performed in dozens of chambara, including classics like *Tsubaki Sanjuro, Seven Samurai,* and *Yojimbo*. Atsuo Nakamura, Katsu Shintaro, Takakura Ken; all these names are those of well-known movies stars in Japan whose films have played in the United States. They are well known in martial arts circles as well, for each of them practices the art of the sword draw, *iaido*. Their budo backgrounds can add a realistic touch to their roles, but each of them will quickly admit that their theatric swordplay is a far cry from the real thing, for several reasons. Among them, the swords used by actors in chambara are not steel, but bamboo, shaped to look like the real thing and covered with a thin veneer of chrome or tin. They weigh only a few ounces, so they can be swung with a rapidity that even the best swordsmen could not hope to equal with a real blade. In addition, fight scenes in chambara are carefully choreographed and rehearsed down to the last detail. The losers know exactly when and how they're to "die," just as the heroes are certain of their "victory."

A duel between the real swordsmen of the feudal era didn't look very much like it is depicted on the screen. Instead, it was usually a blindingly fast second or two, with the winner determined by a fractional advantage in timing. In these encounters, there was no time for intricate movement. Success depended on the simplest of strikes, a straight cut from overhead, or a powerful slash to the side of the body.

The second misconception that may be engendered by a study of the bokken's techniques is the practitioner's belief that he's studying kenjutsu as it was, or is, performed by members of a classical ryu. This is a common and understandable assumption, and few ideas are more inaccurate. In the first place, classical training in the bujutsu is far more severe than most modern budoka in the West are aware of. Secondly, it entails an experience with a number of disciplines not encompassed by the modern martial ways. For example, the classical swordsman had to make a thorough study of human anatomy as it related to his art. He had to know various details of muscle structure and the exact location of the organs, to make his strikes deadly and immediately effective. Further, he could not afford to be skilled only with the sword, for he might, in the course of his career, be forced to face opponents wielding weapons as diverse as spears, clubs, or sickle-and-chains. Most classical ryu curriculum included a study of these weapons, or at least a number of techniques designed to counter them. Other facets of a ryu's teachings included esoteric Buddhist or Shinto lore, and an education in the mythology of Japan as it related to the history and philosophy of the school.

Most importantly, the classical martial artist felt an intimate relationship to his own ryu, and identified himself with it in an intrinsic way. The modern practitioner, no matter how sincere, cannot fully comprehend this emotion, nor will he, unless he makes the effort to join and train in a ryu with roots and traditions centuries old. Currently, both Japan and the West are plagued with a pestilence of ersatz "swordsmen" whose claims of skill are backed only by the ownership of a sword, a marginally likely costume, and instructions gleaned from books. These pitiful imposters invariably claim membership in a ryu, typically a ficitious one, and while their inept handling of the sword reveals their defects as quickly as does their complete lack of understanding of classical martial traditions, they nonetheless perform a dreadful misservice in their charade. Should the sincere practitioner happen across one of these people, he makes every effort to steer clear. What is even more admirable, he resists the egotistic temptation to become one himself.

Suburi is rooted in the techniques of the swordsmanship practiced by the samurai, and most suburi techniques can be found in the basics of the feudal ryu. But suburi techniques are of a very generalized nature. They meet the needs of the modern budoka, who has no practical need for the far more specific methods entailed by the essentials of the ryu, but who wishes nonetheless, to grasp the essentials of the art of the sword as it was followed by the warrior of old.

Once the prospective student of the bokken understands that suburi will enable him neither to duplicate the expertise of filmdom's samurai, nor to claim allegiance to a classical martial arts ryu, he's free to begin training with a minimum of false expectations and misconceived notions. He'll also be able to more readily appreciate the real benefits of using the bokken.

The first of these benefits that will be noticed is in the physical realm. Martial arts teachers and books are fond of pointing out that their particular art is suitable for anyone, regardless of physical condition. It is only fair to warn, though, that suburi is an extremely strenuous exercise. Just the act of swinging the bokken up and down without any force is likely to bring on stiff and sore muscles. This author has conducted seminars on suburi training on occasion, with classes filled with strong karateka or judoka, all young men in their early 20s, black belt holders with the strength and conditioning of professional athletes. Even so, at the end of the session, they were all pitifully tired and sore. "It was like jumping rope," one of them said, "with a lead chain for a rope."

Suburi training involves quick footwork and light, fast body shifting, but it also demands strength and a focusing of physical power, cutting with the bokken in a solid, well-connected movement. Because of this duality, its exercises can be geared for emphasizing whatever specific activity one wishes. There are several movements requiring constant motion in different directions, and these can be performed lightly and smoothly a number of times to increase stamina. Other actions, like the basic cuts and strikes, are simpler, and a great deal of power may be applied in learning them, to develop strength.

It is not the purpose or within the range of this book to detail the complexities of physical fitness. However, after the introduction to suburi it provides, the experienced budoka should be able to gauge his practice with the bokken to achieve whatever results he desires. He will inevitably find strength, agility, timing, and speed improved with it. In this sense, the bokken serves as an excellent form of supplementary exercise for the martial artist, a change of pace from his regular training and a chance to put the lessons of his particular budo to work in an innovative way.

As useful an exercise as suburi training can be, that is a very narrow aspect of it, an exploitation only of its *kyogi,* or purely physical benefits. To grasp a deeper and wider significance, to realize its more lofty aims (*kogi*), it is necessary to examine the spiritual ideals of the sword.

Since its creation, the way of the sword has had a special meaning for the Japanese warrior. This is exemplified in the treatise *Fudo Shinmyo Roku,* the "Record of Immovable Wisdom," written in the mid-1600s by Takuan Soho, a Zen priest who was the friend and religious teacher of Yagyu Munenori no Tajima, perhaps one of the greatest of Japan's swordsmen. Master Yagyu's association with the priest allowed him to realize that swordsmanship was something far beyond the mere techniques of taking a life with his blade.

In his treatise, Takuan explains it: "We have to distinguish between two ways of training, one spiritual, the other practical. The understanding of (technical) principles alone cannot lead one to the mastery of movements. Training is never to be one-sided. Spirit and technique are like two wheels of a cart."

The swordsman whose goals are spiritual in nature never neglects that wheel of the cart. He strives to make the lessons of his training applicable to his daily life, promoting within self-discipline, courage, and equanimity. Approaching his bokken practice as a true form of the budo, he recognizes that self-perfection is the ultimate rationalization for having taken up the weapon. By striking and cutting according to the prescribed movements of suburi, he learns to move almost unconsciously, with complete freedom. By continuing his practice in the face of all manner of obstacles and setbacks, he forges his will and self-reliance. Reflecting on his skills and weaknesses, he gains profound insight into his place in the world.

It is the common goal of all the budo to strive for a spiritual perfection in which benevolence and concern for others is a primary manifestation. That noble attainment, however, is a long and arduous process, which must be incessantly tempered by relentless, hard physical training. Swordmasters like Yagyu Munenori spoke of there being two different kinds of swords. They called one sword—and by extension the swordsman who wielded it—*satsujinken*, merely a weapon for killing, and serving no greater purpose, a "sword that takes life." The *katsujinken,* though, was a "sword that preserved life," promoting dignity and a love for mankind. The use of the katsujinken was in the killing of the worst enemy of all, that of one's own ego.

When training with the bokken, the serious student should try to make every blow as if it were actually cutting down an opponent. He should, at the same time, however, bear in mind that the highest purpose of his cutting is not at an enemy outside himself, but at the ego inspired pretensions and inadequacies that lurk within. The never-ending process of attacking these internal enemies is called *kirihaku*, to "cut at the impurities" within the self. If he is very determined, very dedicated, and very fortunate, after many years of experience, the modern swordsman may look back and realize with satisfaction, that this fight is the only really worthy goal of taking up the bokken.

Zarei (Seated Bow)

The budoka begins and ends his training sessions with bows to the dojo, to the memory of the masters who've gone before, and to his opponent.

If you seek mastery of the sword, seek
first sincerity of the heart, for the former
is but a reflection of the latter.
    —Iwakura Yoshinori, of Yagyu-ryu

SELECTING THE BOKKEN
AND EQUIPMENT

Among the treasured possessions of the Matsui family of Japan are two wooden swords, made of a dark, ebony-like wood, believed to have belonged to Miyamoto Musashi. Resting on a stand specially made for them, they glow, seemingly with a warm, inner light. Without even touching them, their balance and weight are apparent. Carved like a work of art, they are as beautiful as the finest steel sword, curving gently down the length of the blade and rounded to a smooth oval to fit perfectly into the swordsman's grip. They are an excellent example of the combination of practicality and beauty that is to be found in the bokken.

The wooden sword used in suburi training can be constructed of a variety of woods, and may be called by different names. Originally, it is a bokken or *bokuto.* Both mean literally and simply "wooden blade." However, one may hear the weapon referred to as a *suburito, kaisuburito, hakusuburito,* or *jigen suburito.* Suburito, of course, means the sword "*to*" for suburi. (Depending upon the character used to write it, the word for sword can be pronounced "to" or "ken.") The prefixes of *kai* and *haku* are references to the exact size and shape of the bokken. *Jigen* refers to a particular kind of bokken used by students of the Jigen-ryu, a kendo/kenjutsu style of fencing from Kyushu, in southern Japan. Since the jigen sword is heavier than most other bokken, it is sometimes favored by swordsmen of other styles for practice.

In general, a distinction is made between the bokken and the suburito, in that the latter is much thicker at the "blade" part of the weapon than it is at the handle. This gives, considerably more weight to the suburito than is found in the bokken. The suburito is ideal for practicing basics and simpler movements, but it is rarely used in the two-man exercises of *kata* (prearranged forms).

The two most common woods used to make bokken are Japanese red *(aka)* or white *(shiroi)* oak *(kunugi),* both of which have a close grain and allow a smooth, blemish-free finish. Because the red oak tends to warp less in the climates of the Occident than does the white, it's become more widely used outside Japan. It's the opinion of some practitioners, though, that white oak makes a superior bokken in that the grain is finer, less likely to contain knots, and is a bit sturdier than its red cousin. White oak bokken are typically more expensive and usually must be bought directly from Japanese suppliers.

Although oak is the most popular wood from which bokken are carved, it is not the only species used, by any means. Ebony, a hard, dark wood that's an Asian relative of the persimmon is sometimes made into bokken, producing a high-quality weapon that is almost unbreakable. Another nearly indestructible bokken is made of Japanese sunuke. During the feudal age, bokken were frequently made from *biwa,* a wood resembling cypress that grows in the mountains of central Japan. While biwa bokken are also quite durable and heavy, they were wielded with care during practice by many swordsmen, and others refused to use them at all. The reason has to do with a folk superstition of the time, which persists today among some rural martial artists in that country, that a bruise or other injury inflicted by biwa would not heal, and the wound would eventually kill the swordsman.

In the past few years, American budoka have begun to experiment with a variety of North American hardwoods to make bokken, with impressive results. Hickory, persimmon, ironwood, and walnut all produce very good weapons. Yet, unless the student is skilled in woodworking, it's easier to purchase a bokken through a martial arts equipment supplier, either in the U.S. or Japan. That transaction can be a shock for even the most stalwart of budoka, for with the popularity of swordsmanship, the price of bokken is suddenly rivaling that of Queen Anne furniture. It isn't unheard of for bokken to fetch $40-50, and some cost even more. Recently a bokken made of a rare South American wood was advertised for $200, a bit extravagant considering that, aesthetics aside, what we're talking about here is a piece of wood the size of a walking stick. Actually, these prices reflect more the appeal of fashion or the exotic, not to mention the entreprenurial ambitions of the suppliers, than they do need for such expensive weapons. Beginner and master alike can suffice with an ordinary oak bokken which, while it may eventually break under years of hard use, is replaced for a modest price more in keeping with the simple ways of the martial artist.

A note of warning, though, must be made regarding the selection of a bokken. Many wooden swords are now made in Taiwan, from a cheaper, much lighter kind of reddish wood that has few of the qualities of the real thing. These bokken can be distinguished easily by the wood's wide, poor grain and their light, poorly balanced feel. They are not sturdy enough to be adequate for suburi, shattering under the firm blows dealt in practice. While their price is attractive, it is essential to get a bokken that will stand up under harsh training.

No matter what wood the bokken is made from, it requires very little care. Often bokken today are varnished, but if not, it's a good idea to rub tung oil into the entire surface of the weapon a couple of times a year, to keep the wood from drying out. Other than that, a natural finish will be given to it by constant use. Always store the bokken in a dry place, preferably in some way to keep it from warping. Just before, and even during a strenuous practice session with the bokken, it's wise to run one's hand up and down the blade, to insure that contact with an opponent's weapon hasn't splintered it. If the bokken is damaged, it should be replaced immediately.

The bokken should always be thought of as a real weapon. In fact, with the exception just mentioned, of running the hand up and down the blade to check for damage, it should always be treated and handled as if it were a sharp katana. This attitude encourages the seriousness of purpose that will set the practitioner on the correct path toward mastery.

Among traditional swordsmen, it's believed that something of the practitioner's spirit and feeling is transferred to the bokken. Through long training, the weapon acquires a special feel, reflecting the balance and coordination of the user. Therefore, to be allowed to use a master's bokken during training is an honor and should be considered so. Likewise, one should never let another handle his own, or use another student's bokken without permission. Perhaps such considerations may be esoteric, but they were part of the daily weave of the classical warrior's behavior and they should be maintained devotedly if one is to make the way of the sword his own.

Ideally, the student of the bokken will have access to a dojo with a wooden floor for his practice. Lacking that, however, he may use any place convenient, provided it is clean, with a smooth floor, and a modicum of privacy. It's both interesting and necessary, when weather permits, to train out of doors, in different settings. This allows the student to perfect his movements on uneven terrain and exposes him to other conditions not found in the dojo that will be helpful in his training.

Just as it is not necessary to have a formal dojo in which to train, neither is it necessary to wear any special clothing for his practice with the bokken. It's probable, though, that he'll wish to acquire the uniform traditionally worn by students of the sword. It consists of the following:

A *uwagi* (heavy, twill cotton jacket) like those worn by aikidoka and judoka. It's possible to wear the lighter karate-type jacket as well. Customarily, the uwagi is white, unless worn by a highly ranked exponent, who wears a dark blue or black jacket. If the uwagi has ties, they should be knotted securely, to prevent the lapels from pulling open during training.

The *obi* (belt) is wrapped around the waist, to keep the jacket closed and to give a cinched feel about the hips that encourages the swordsman to maintain a firm body connection. The obi is a wide strip of cloth several feet long, wrapped around the body and tied in the rear. The knot provides a sort of bustle that pulls the *hakama* up in the back, so the wearer is prevented from tripping on its hem.

Of course, there are no ranks in suburi training, and the color of the belt, typically white or black, is immaterial.

The *joba hakama* is a split skirt, or pleated trousers, of the kind worn by men in Japan during the feudal era. It's now worn by men and women who practice aikido, kendo, iaido, and kyudo. Black, dark blue, or white, it has a rigid halter (*koshi ita*) in the rear, and straps that are tied front and back to secure it about the waist. The hakama's hem should reach to a point almost two inches from the floor when standing, striking the leg just at the middle of the ankle. When cleaning the dojo, or training outside in wet weather, the legs of the hakama are tucked up into the waistband. In the days of the samurai, pulling up one's hakama was called *momodachi,* and was a clear indication that one intended to fight. To help keep the hakama neat and orderly, it's advisable to wear a pair of white cotton pants (*zubon*) underneath, like those worn in the judo or karate.

It should go without saying that the uniform must be kept immaculate. Training outside, or during the warmer months will soil it, but jacket and pants should be washed after every practice and left to air out. The hakama will need less frequent laundering (when done, it should be washed by hand), but it should be kept carefully folded and aired out between training sessions.

Sword and mind must be united.
Technique by itself is insufficient,
and spirit alone is not enough.
—Yamada Jirokichi, of Jikishinkage-ryu

KIHON
(Basics and Fundamentals)

All your efforts in suburi training will be for naught if the most basic fundamentals are neglected. It is safe to say that these—holding the bokken correctly, stance and posture and body movement while striking—are the foundations of any expertise or sophistication of technique that may follow. Without them, any advancement will be flawed. Unfortunately, it is today common to see even very highly ranked martial artists handling a bokken in a way that, should it actually be used in combat, would produce only the most negligible results. The same may be said for posture and body movement. If you, on the other hand, study these fundamentals carefully and follow their lessons exactly, you will find your skill and ability noticeably improved later on.

Gripping the Bokken

There is only one proper way to hold the bokken. The grip should give the feeling of squeezing quite firmly with the little and ring fingers of both hands, with the remaining fingers and both thumbs merely guiding the bokken. There must be a firmness in the wrists, but no tenseness.

Left Hand

(1) Starting with the left hand, take the very bottom of the handle in the palm. (2) Beginning with the little finger, close the fingers around the handle in a snug grip. (3) It is important that the little finger not actually be wrapped around the weapon itself, but curled tightly beneath it. The left thumb should be wrapped around the ring finger.

Right Hand

(1) The right hand grips the bokken tilted at a slight upward angle, (2) with each of the fingers wrapped around the handle just below where the sword's guard would be. With the right hand grip, the thumb should be across the middle finger and the right forefinger should be extended naturally along the shaft of the bokken.

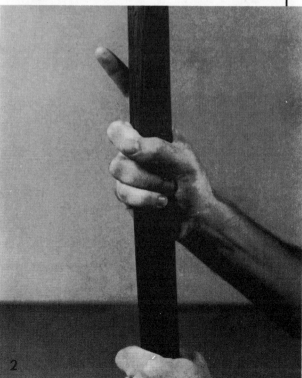

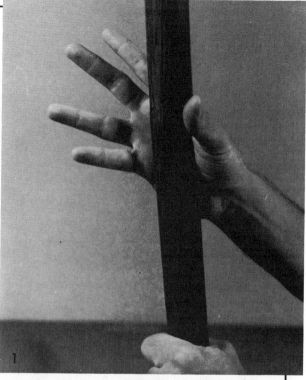

Proper Grip

The proper grip is essential for productive training for several reasons. (A) With the left little finger curled under the bokken, you will find you have a greater range of motion vertically than you would find otherwise. (B) With the right forefinger pointing, the bokken immediately feels more like an extension of the arm, and the weapon is more closely connected to the rest of the body. (C) With wrists aligned, the joints can absorb the shock of striking and little stress is placed on them or the shoulders.

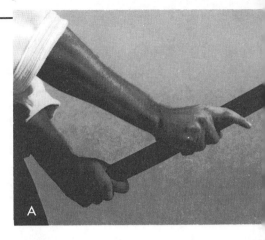

Incorrect Grips

Incorrect grips (A&B), with wrists bent in, or out, or (C) with the hands too close together, will all impede proper motion and actions with the bokken, and can result in injury.

Getting the Right Feel

(A&B) In gripping the bokken, make sure it extends at a slight angle upward from the center of the body, about a hand-span below the navel. It is the tendency of the beginner to hold the sword too tightly, reducing flexibility and strength. Often, (C) more advanced suburi practitioners are seen to grip their weapons so lightly that their fingers are loose and extended in mid-strike. This looseness will be difficult, if not impossible for the beginner, but it gives an idea of the right feeling.

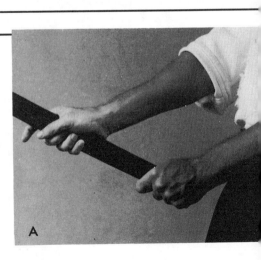

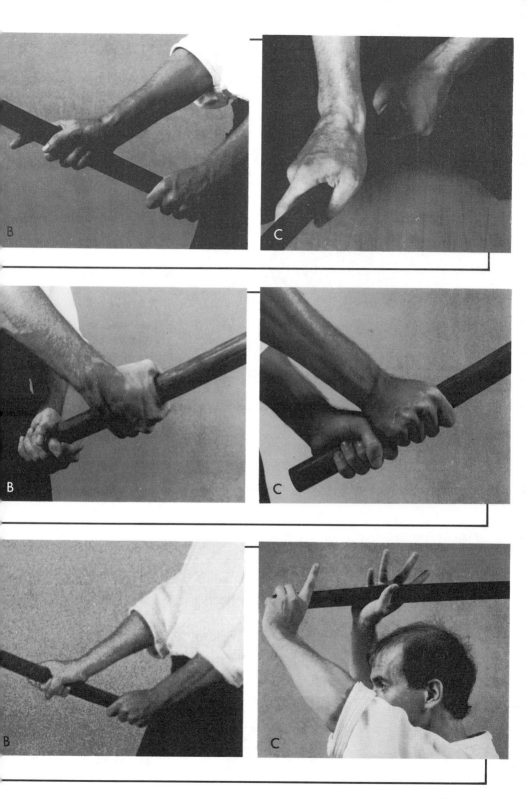

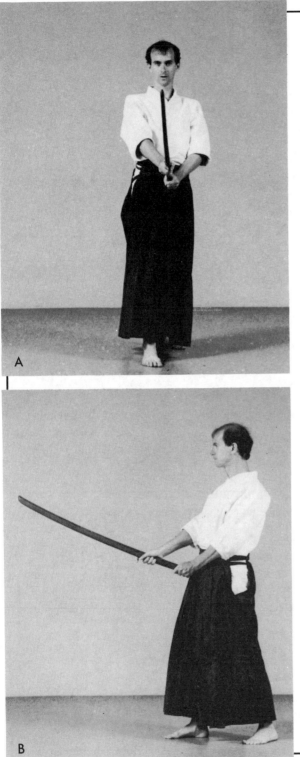

A

B

THE BASIC STANCE

Sankakudai
—Basic Suburi Stance

The most frequently used posture in suburi training is (A) *sankakudai*, a "triangular" stance that permits quick, controlled movement in multiple directions. All kamae in suburi training are executed from sankakudai. (B) The feet are positioned

Left Side View

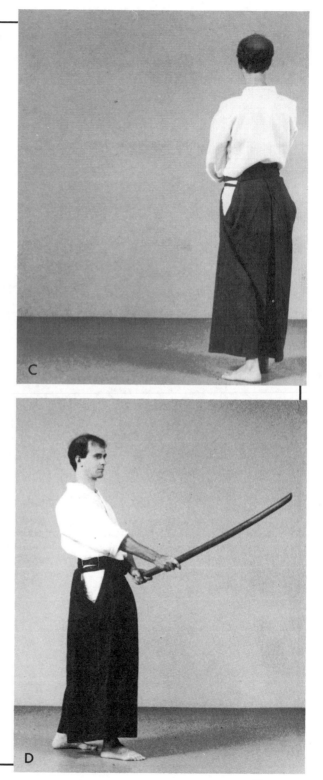

slightly wider apart than shoulder width. (C) The back foot is turned out at about a 45-degree angle, and (D) the front foot is pointed straight ahead. Care should be taken to center the body evenly, and to tighten the muscles of the hips and buttocks.

Right Side View

A

Incorrect Suburi Stances

(A) Note that if the rear foot is turned at too great an angle, body weight and balance are affected. (B) Lifting the rear heel is a stance taken in kendo, permitting rapid movement forward and back, but which inhibits angular motion. (C) Too wide a stance will not permit fast movement. Karate stances such as *zenkutsu dachi* and *kiba dachi* are not related to the art of the sword, and are not used in training.

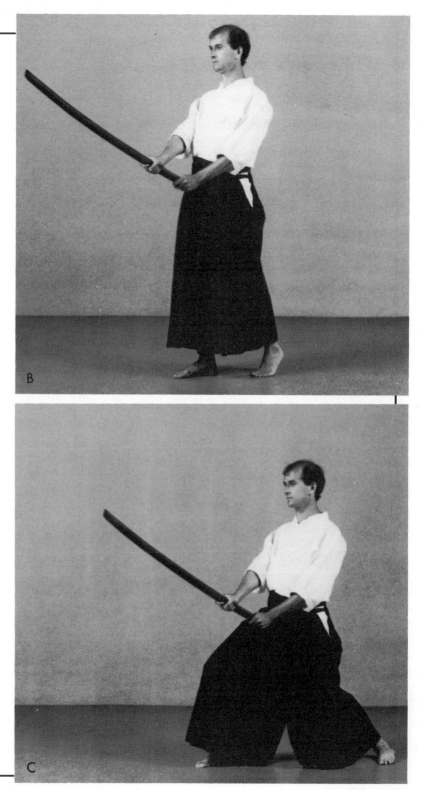

B

C

BOKKEN POSITIONS

Chudan Kamae
(Middle Level Position)

The fundamental kamae for suburi is that of the chudan. The feeling should be one of pushing forward slightly, with the buttocks firm, and shoulders low and relaxed. (A) Seeing it from the front, notice that the bokken is positioned so the hilt extends upward at the correct angle from just below the navel. (B) From the left side, note the angle, and that the sword is pointed at an imaginary opponent's throat. In chudan kamae, the butt of the bokken is kept at about fist's width away from the body. (Y) One common error is angling the bokken too low for proper chudan.

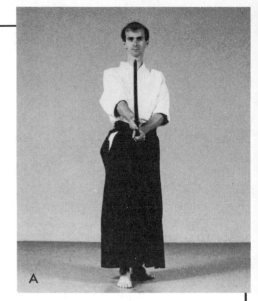

Front View

Side View

**Incorrect
Chudan Kamae**

A

Jodan Kamae
(Upper Level Position)

Jodan kamae requires (A) the bokken to be held in a horizontal posture above the head, parallel to the ground. The most important point in mastering jodan kamae is the placement of the elbows. (B) Try to keep them flexed naturally, to provide a light kind of springiness, with the hands steady, just in front of the forehead. (C) Although the hips remain facing fully to the front in jodan, the upper body is twisted slightly to keep the bokken in a direct midline of the body's upper trunk.

B

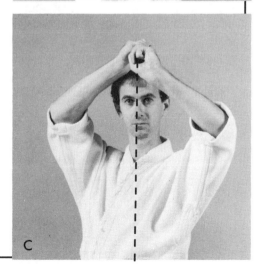

C

47

Incorrect Jodan Kamae

(A) Take care not to hold the hilt too high, but keep it about level with the forehead. (B) Your elbows must not be too close to your body, or (C) too wide away from your body. (D&E) A common fault in jodan is holding the bokken in a position that is not horizontal.

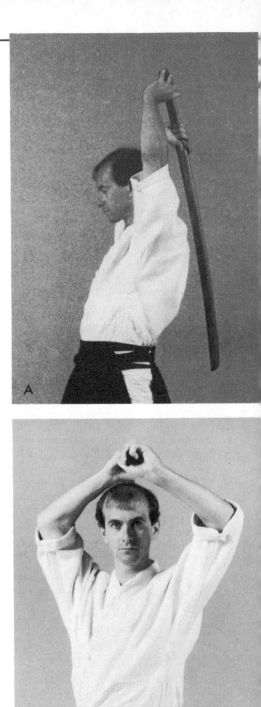

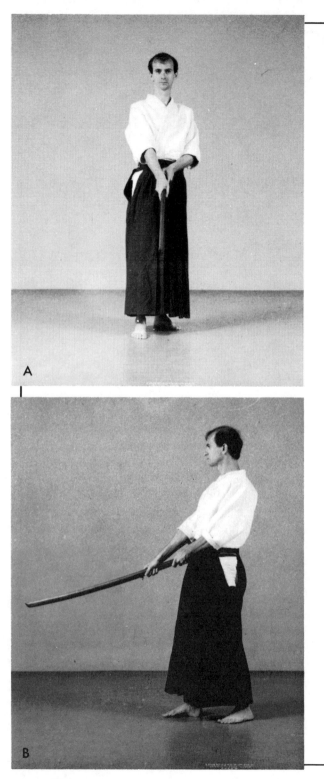

Gedan Kamae
(Lower Level Position)

Gedan kamae calls for (A) the bokken to be lowered from the middle level position. (B) Hips should be rocked forward slightly, with the tip of the bokken sloping down in a natural posture from the wrists. *Note:* Do not hold the bokken with the wrists bent unnaturally or hands too close to the body.

Side View

Other Subri Kamae

There are many other kamae. In fact, most feudal ryu have kamae that are particular to their style. For basic suburi practice, only two other kamae besides jodan, chudan and gedan are necessary. These are hasso kamae and waki kamae.

Right Hasso Kamae

Left Hasso Kamae

Right Waki Kamae

Left Waki Kamae

TAI SABAKI
(Body Movement)

Tsugi Ashi (Sliding Step)

Tsugi ashi is known by a variety of names. It is one of the stablest ways of advancing while constantly maintaining the sankakudai stance. (1) Begin in sankakudai, with the right foot leading. (2&3) Without moving the right foot, slide the left foot forward. When it is about a foot's distance beyond the right, begin turning the right foot outward. In making tsugi ashi, try to keep the balls of both feet sliding along the ground, and as the rear foot rotates outward, turn it on the ball of the foot, and not on the heel. By the time the left foot has advanced a stance length, the right (which is now the rear foot), will have rotated outward to assume a left sankakudai. Then, (4-7) repeat the same movements as you step with the other foot, and so on. Notice that the hips, shoulders, and bokken all remain stable and steady through the stepping.

SIDE VIEW

1

SIDE VIEW

3

6

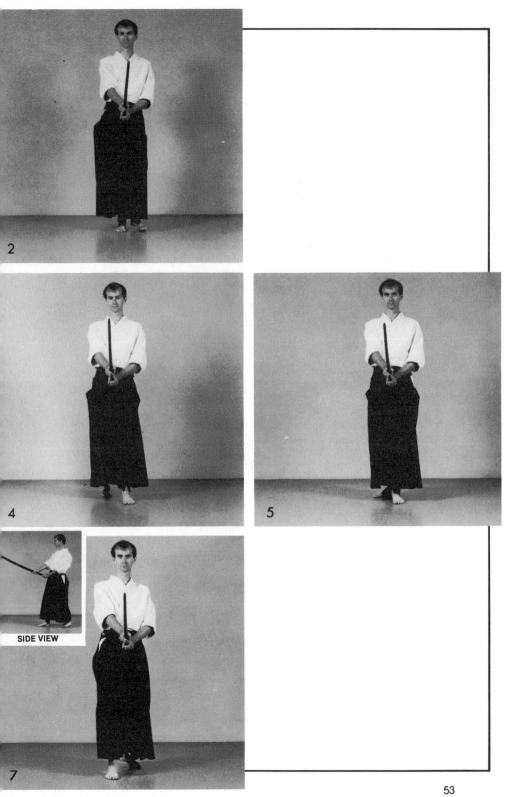

SIDE VIEW

2

4

5

7

Naname Okuri Ashi
(Oblique Advancing Step)

Naname okuri ashi is made by (1) starting in chudan. (2&3) Step forward smoothly with the right foot at about a 45-degree angle to the front, with the left foot sliding up to regain the original stance width. (4) To step forward into a left advancing step, begin in a right chudan, then (5) step forward with the left leg leading, at an angle towards the left of front. No matter which foot leads when practicing okuri ashi, try to imagine an opponent stepping in and striking down at your head. Your movement to the side should be just enough to elude his strike, still leaving you in the position to make a counterattack. It is most important to keep the hips moving smoothly and to keep the bokken in a chudan position throughout the movement. Do not raise or lower the body center during okuri ashi.

1

3

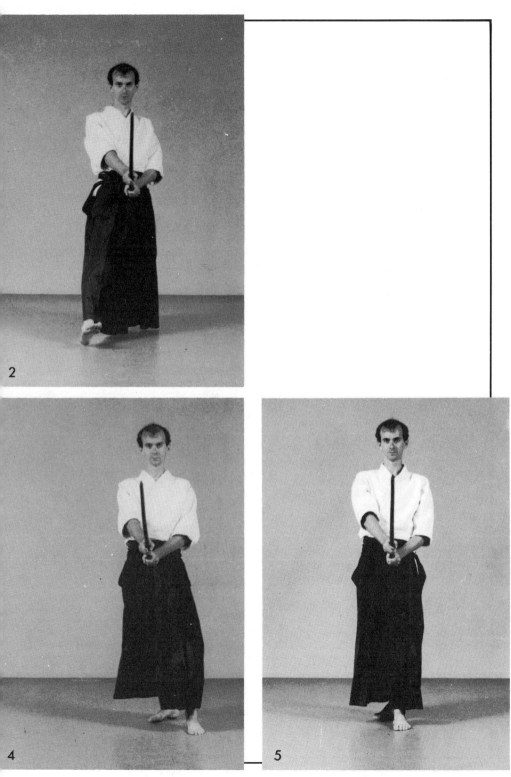

2

4

5

Assuming Iaigoshi
(Crouching Position)

During the warrior age in Japan, people sat on matted floors. And so, the samurai developed a kind of crouch which allowed them to maintain a stance of readiness at all times. This posture is called iaigoshi. To assume iaigoshi, (1) begin in chudan. (2) Drop down to kneel on the left knee, bending back the toes of the left foot. (3) Pull the bent right leg back slightly at an angle.

1

Iaigoshi

(A) It is important to keep the balls of both feet on a line, and (B&C) to keep the hips slightly higher than the right knee. Injury can result if the forward knee is bent too deeply and allowed to remain above the center of balance in the hips.

A

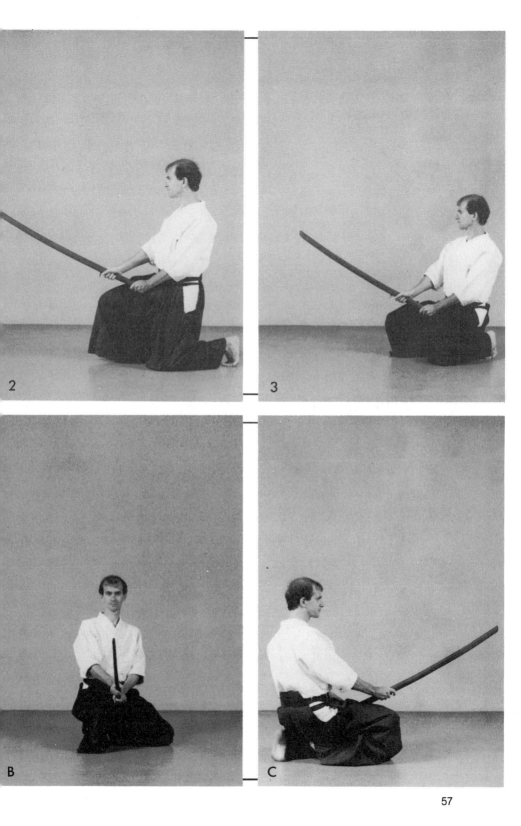

2

3

B

C

Shikko (Crouching Walk)

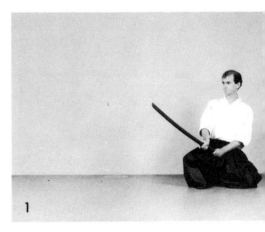

From iaigoshi, you must be able to move quickly in shikko. At first, iaigoshi may be uncomfortable and shikko will be painful and awkward. With practice, however, it is possible to sit in iaigoshi for long periods without discomfort and to move as quickly across the floor in shikko as you can walk. Be patient and work slowly. To move forward in shikko (1&2) drop the right knee to the floor and, (3) without raising the hips, step forward to assume a left-leg-leading iaigoshi. (4-7) Repeat the movement to continue moving forward in a straight line. While moving in shikko, keep the balls of the feet in a straight line and avoid raising and lowering the body. Shikko may be done without the bokken, with the hands resting on the thighs, but practicing it with the weapon held in chudan position is excellent for improving kamae and posture.

Shikko Turning

To turn 180 degrees in shikko, (1&2) proceed to move forward in shikko, then (3&4) as you bring your left foot forward, begin to turn by pivoting on the balls of both feet. (5-7) As you complete your 180-degree turn, begin moving back in the opposite direction in shikko.

3

6

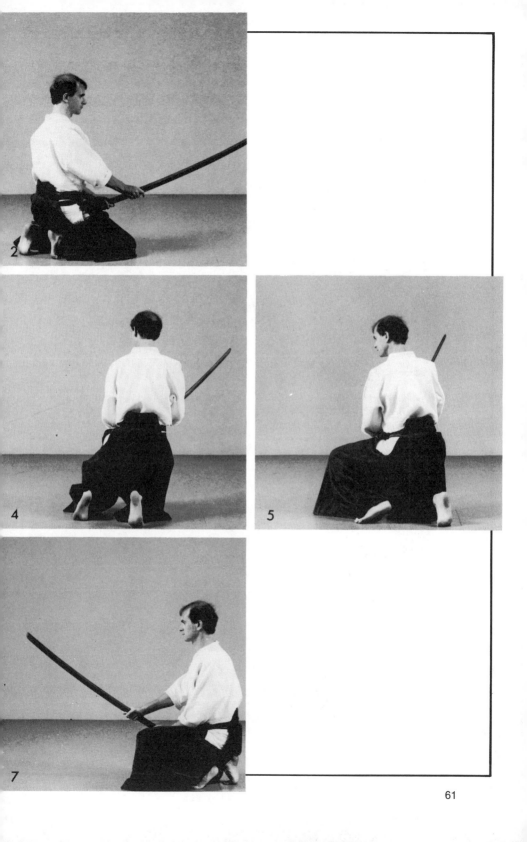

Do not concentrate on striking your opponent. Maintain yourself naturally, like moonbeams flooding into a leaky cottage.

. . . . . .

Don't hold back trying to protect your ass. As soon as an opening appears, sieze it!

—Yamaoka Tesshu, of Muto-ryu

UCHI KATA
(Striking Methods)

There are six basic methods of striking in suburi training: *Shomen uchi* (straight overhead), *hidari* and *migi naname* (left and right diagonal), *hidari* and *migi yoko uchi* (left and right side), and *tsuki* (thrust). At the beginning of your training, simply try to find the correct action without worrying about developing power. It is vital not to lose your form at any time during the strike. Later, as the movements are learned, you should try to slowly concentrate the strike so that it stops exactly where you intend it, without wavering. A good way to practice all the basic strikes is to train outdoors, near a tree with low hanging branches. Slowly cut down at a single leaf or branch, stopping the bokken just before contact. Gradually increase the speed of the strike until it is possible to cut at full force, focusing the action so that it stops at precisely the right instant. It is advisable to make all strikes focused at the chudan, or middle level, as they are shown here. As progress is made, you may try to stop your cuts at higher and lower targets.

Shomen Uchi
(Cutting Down)

(1) From the right chudan (2&3), step straight forward, simultaneously raising the bokken to jodan level. Continue the step, (4) bringing the bokken down in a line that reverses exactly its upward path, in front of the body. (5) The step is completed at the same time the bokken is focused at the

completion of the cut. Try to finish the strike with the feet once again in the same san-kakudai stance in which they started, neither closer together nor farther apart. This method of stepping is exactly like that of naname okuri ashi, except that the movement is straight to the front rather than at an angle.

Shomen Uchi
with Tsugi Ashi

Shomen uchi should also be performed while stepping forward in tsugi ashi. (1) Starting in chudan (2) step forward, raising the bokken to jodan. When moving forward to strike with the bokken, the advancing foot describes a shallow inward arc on the floor, bringing both knees almost in contact as they brush by. At this moment, (3) the bokken should be directly in the jodan position. Any variance in this timing will affect the timing of the whole strike. (4&5) Continue, bringing the bokken down.

SIDE VIEW

1

3

SIDE VIEW

SIDE VIEW

SIDE VIEW

5

Shomen Uchi with
Tsugi Ashi—Rear View

(1-7) Remember to maintain proper jodan position when the sword is brought above the head. Do not let it drift farther back, or neglect to bring it into the proper posture before cutting. Also notice that the rear leg, as it steps forward, swings in to brush the other leg, then swings out again as it stops in front.

1

4

5

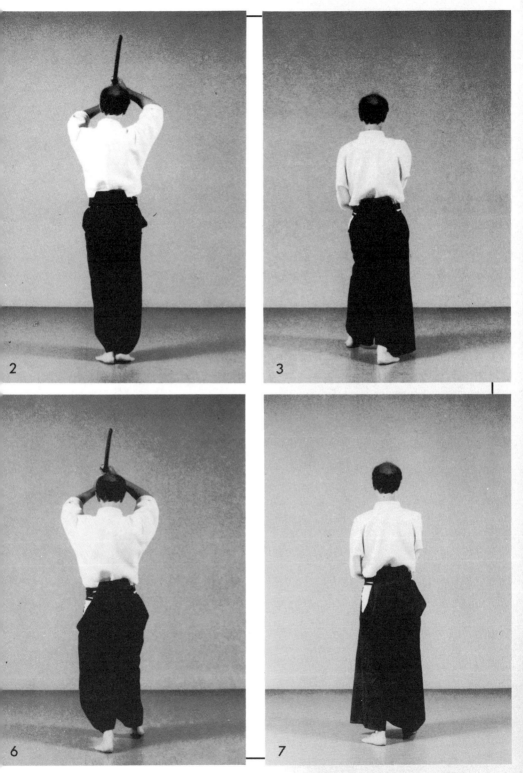

Shomen Uchi—
Moving to the Rear

Shomen uchi should be practiced while moving to the rear, in which case, the movements are simply reversed. A common error when moving backward is to lose tight body connection, allowing the hips to stick out. (1-3) Raise the bokken into jodan as you bring your front leg back, swinging it inward at the same time to brush your other leg. (4-6) Continue stepping back, swinging your leg back out to the side slightly, and striking down with the bokken as you complete your backward step.

1

4

2

3

5

6

Naname Giri
(Cutting at an Angle)

Cutting with the bokken at an angle is naname giri. Originally, different schools of swordsmanship had a wide variety of ways to accomplish this strike. Some directed the sword against the tip of the opponent's shoulder, while others made the angle narrower, aimed at the base of the neck. For the purposes of suburi training, naname giri is made as if one were cutting down on a line that is the same angle as that formed by the outer lapel of the training jacket. To make naname giri, (1) begin in the chudan position and (2) step forward, raising the sword in the same line as if making an overhead cut. (3) Cant the sword slightly to the left side as it begins to come down and (4) cut down smoothly. (5) The bokken should stop at the chudan position, but with the blade turned at an angle.

1

3

Naname Giri with Tsugi Ashi

Like shomen uchi, naname giri should be practiced with the front foot leading each time, and with tsugi ashi. When learning the technique, (1) return the blade to the vertical chudan position before the next strike. After proficiency is gained, it is possible to make repetitions continuously, without pausing to readjust between strikes. It is also important to (2) raise the bokken along the same line of angle that it will descend. When moving forward (3) cut down on the left as you step with your left foot, and (4-6) cut down on the right as you step with your right. Make sure the weapon comes up along the same path it descended before making the next strike.

1

4

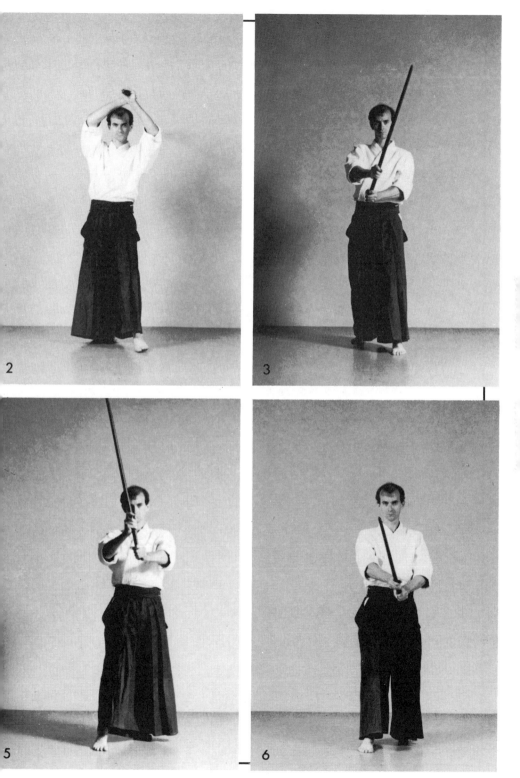

Yoko Uchi (Side Strike)

The yoko uchi, or horizontal strike requires a more sophisticated body movement than is found in either shomen uchi or naname giri. Because the bokken is swung in a flat, horizontal direction, there is a tendency among beginners to lose control of the stroke, resulting in an unfocused, baseball-bat-like swing. Instead, yoko uchi must be as controlled and focused as the other strikes, and the way to achieve this is through incessant practice. (1) Starting in the right chudan position, (2) bring the bokken up in a circular movement that begins with the step forward. (3&4) The movement continues as the bokken passes overhead, (5&6) following

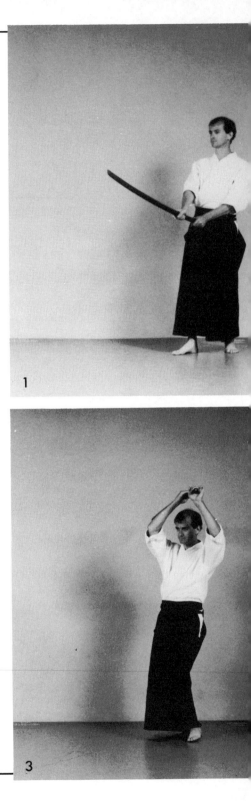

1

3

Continued

6

through as the weapon is brought to a horizontal cutting plane and until it is stopped along the midline of the body, with the blade in a flat position. (7-10) As with the other strikes, when the movement is reversed and repeated on the other side, the bokken follows the same path.

8

7

10

Reverse Yoko Uchi

When learning yoko uchi, it is best to cut so the bokken is swung in the same direction as the foot is advancing. Therefore, if the left foot is stepping forward, the cut is directed from the left to right. As skill increases, the student can reverse this order, performing *gyaku* (reverse yoko uchi). Because yoko uchi generates such

1

2

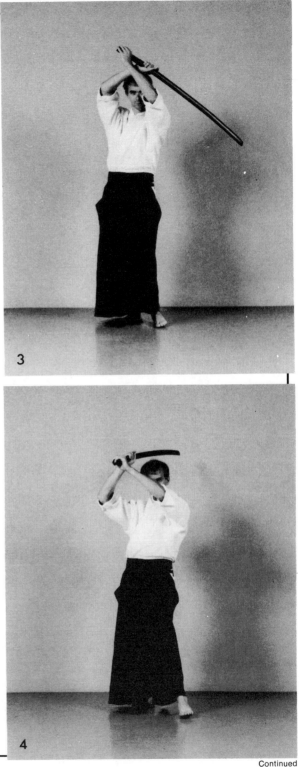

force and momentum, it is a very powerful blow. Swordsmen during the feudal era were capable of cutting entirely through a human being using it. However, it requires lengthy practice to control the bokken during the strike. At the beginning of yoko uchi, (1-4) both hips and shoulders rotate in the direction of the cut. At the

3

4

Continued

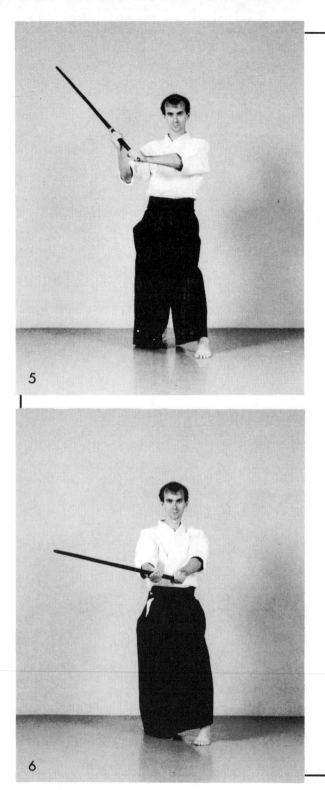

5

6

moment of focus, though, (5-8) the shoulders must remain locked into position, while the hips must reverse snappily, insuring correct force. This can only be gained through repetition of technique.

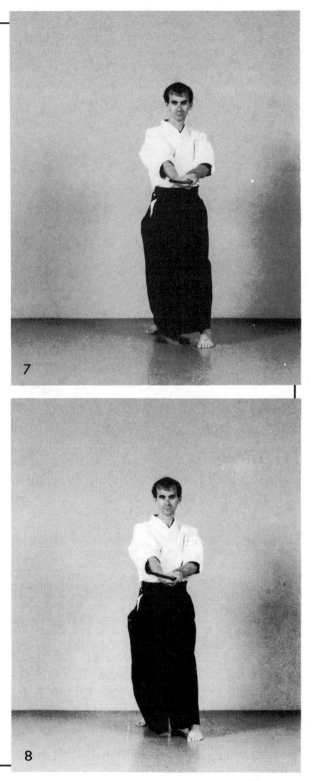

7

8

1

2

3A

3

Tsuki (Thrusting)—
First Method

Unlike most European bladed weapons, the Japanese sword is not predominantly a thrusting weapon. However, thrusting, or tsuki, with the bokken should not be overlooked, since it is especially designed to take advantage of the curvature of the sword itself. Tsuki is perhaps the most difficult strike in suburi training, because there is little room for a "windup." The swordsman must generate power in a straight line, and deliver it with force and focus. This power is generated through relaxing the shoulders and upper body at the moment before the strike, then strengthening them at the instant of it. Tsuki should be practiced two ways, the first involving stepping forward with alternate legs, thrusting with each step, and returing to chudan kamae in between each thrust. To practice tsuki, (1) assume right chudan. (2) Rotating the bokken so the blade is turning to the right, step forward with the left leg. (3) Continue to turn the bokken until the step is completed, when the weapon should be turned parallel to the ground. Your stance is somewhat wider than at the completion of other strikes. To make correct tsuki, it is necessary to (3A) rotate the wrists. (4) Return to chudan kamae, then (5&6) step forward with the right leg this time, and thrust as before. Remember to keep the forefinger of the right hand pointing in the direction of the thrust. It is also important not to lunge into the thrust. Instead, keep the shoulders back and the hands no further away from the trunk of the body than in the regular chudan position.

4

5

6

1

Tsuki—Second Method

The second method of practicing tsuki is to make shomen uchi, stepping in, followed by a step and thrust. (1) Start in right chudan. (2-4) Step forward and strike with shomen uchi. (5) Pause momentarily, and relax the shoulders. It can be seen that the bokken is pulled toward the body just slightly in between strikes. This allows momentum for the thrust. As practice continues, try to make this pause shorter and smoother, integrating it into the series of movements. Then (6) step forward with the alternate leg and (7) thrust. For practice's sake, no matter which leg is advanced during the thrust, turn the bokken so the blade is facing to the right.

3

6

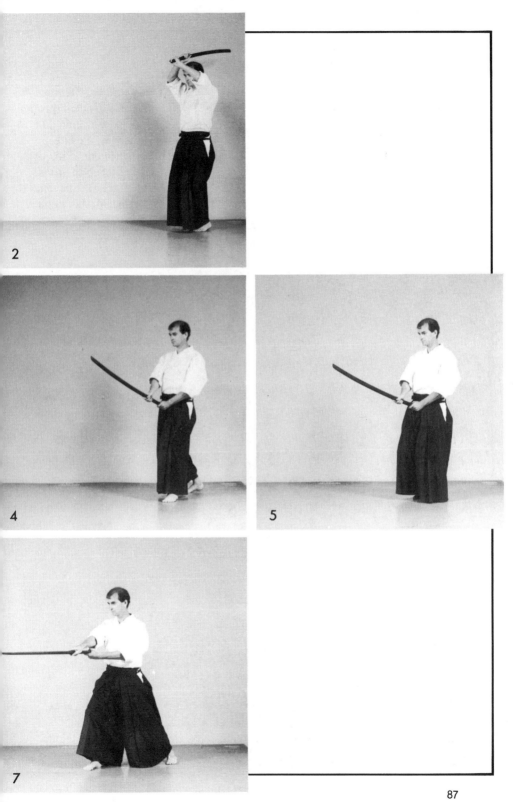

Other Striking Methods

As the student progresses in his training, he will become aware of many different kinds of striking techniques. Most of these are beyond the scope of this book, but three will be presented that utilize the kamae

Shomen Uchi from Gedan Kamae

(1) Start in right gedan kamae. (2-4) Step forward with the right leg, raising the bokken to jodan in a rapid movement. (5&6) Continuing the step, strike down in shomen uchi. The feeling of the

described in an earlier section. These methods of striking are advanced, and require coordination and a thorough understanding of basics. They serve here as examples of the variety of techniques in suburi practice.

first part of this strike is one of cutting up with the point of the bokken as it is raised. There can be no hesitation in lifting the sword or in striking down.

Naname Giri from Hasso Kamae

(1) Beginning in the right side hasso kamae, (2&3) step forward and bring the bokken down (4-6) to make naname giri. When striking from hasso kamae it is very difficult not to "telegraph" the strike by making small movements just before the cut. The action must be instantaneous and direct.

1

4

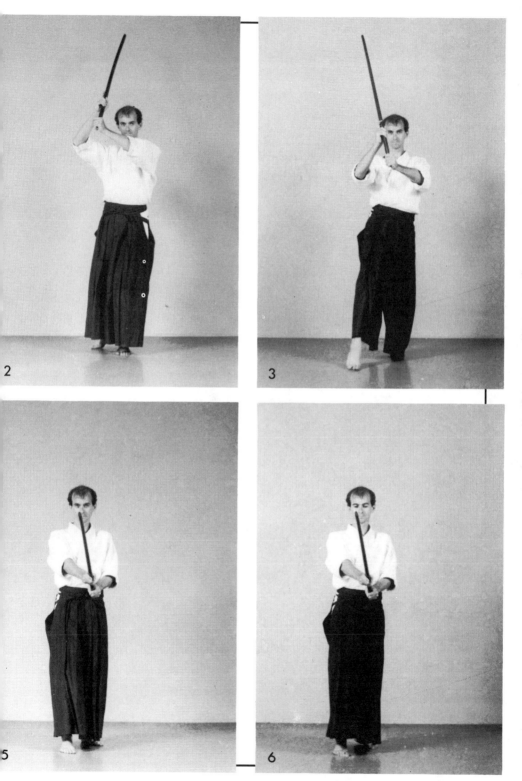

2

3

5

6

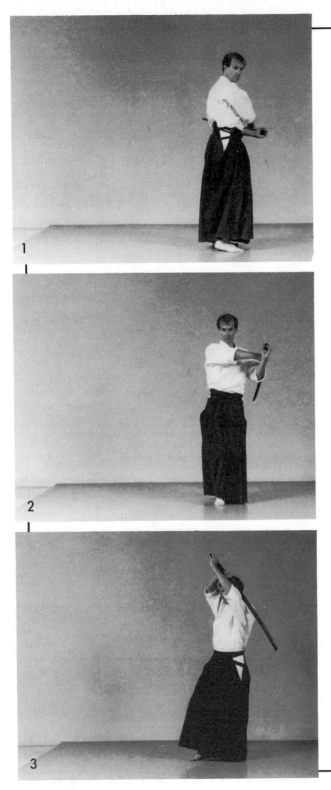

Shomen Uchi from Waki Kamae

(1) From a left waki kamae, (2) pivot to the right, carrying the bokken through a whipping motion (3&4) to an overhead position. Raise the bokken smoothly as you turn. (5) Step forward as you complete the 90-degree turn

to the right, and (6) cut down with shomen uchi. Be sure to make your motion from waki kamae to shomen uchi one continuous cutting motion; and during execution, keep the bokken at the correct distance from the body.

93

You must understand spirit and timing.
Handle the sword naturally, and move
your limbs in accord with your spirit.
  —Miyamoto Musashi, of Niten Ichi-ryu

RENRAKU WAZA
(Combination Techniques)

Once the basic strikes have been correctly learned, they may be put into combinations or renraku waza. The purpose of renraku waza might be thought to be that of increasing one's ability to make a number of strikes to defeat an opponent. This, however, is unsound reasoning, and should you approach this facet of suburi with that as your primary objective, you will be disappointed. Instead, try very hard when practicing combination techniques, to be aware of body shifting and balance. Observe posture and balance, not just during the execution of the strikes, but in the intervals *between* them as well. If there is a gap in balance, mentally or physically, the meaning of the combination is lost. Always bear in mind that the average swordsman can deliver an effective strike within a reasonable amount of training time. It is a mark of distinction of the advanced student of the bokken, though, that he can deliver any number of them, in consecutive order, shifting in any direction and striking at any angle necessary. Thus, the primary objective of training in combination techniques is not to practice the strike themselves, but to teach the body to shift, contract, and expand, at will.

Kiriage (Upward Slash) and Naname Giri

Kiriage, which is known also by many different names, is one of the techniques of suburi training which has some obvious relation to the combat-oriented disciplines of swordsmanship. It is extremely effective for moving the body out of the way of an attack, parrying it, and putting the swordsman at the same time into an advantageous position to make an attack of his own. (1) Begin in chudan kamae. (2) Step forward and out at an angle towards your left, turning the bokken towards the right at the same time. (3) Allow the sword to follow a natural path up and over your head as you (4&5) continue to step forward, finally cutting down in naname giri.

1

3

2

4

5

1

Kiriage and Naname Giri
—Another Angle

Viewed from the side, the "whippy" action of the bokken during kiriage is better observed. (1-4) You should have the feeling of parrying an overhead attack during the first part of the combination, and of simultaneously cutting upward with the blade. Care should be taken not to tilt or lean with the upper body during any part of the action. (5-8) Cut down in naname giri.

3

6

1

2

Kiriage and Naname Giri —Advanced Version

A more advanced version of kiriage involves the same actions, but (1&2) it is performed while moving at an angle. (3) At the middle of the slide to the rear, both feet should be close togeth-

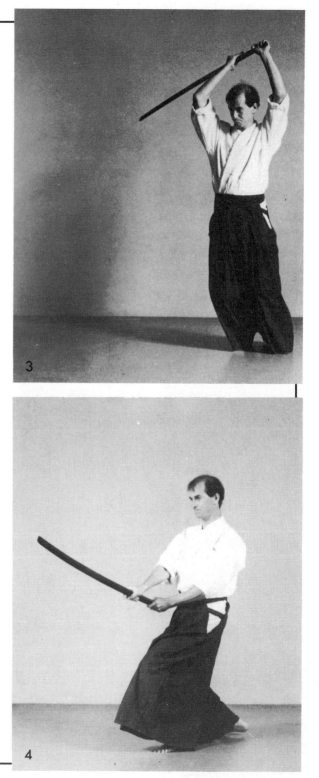

er, with the weight already shifting forward. This form of kiriage creates a different kind of dodge and establishes an effective distancing before (4) the counterattack is made.

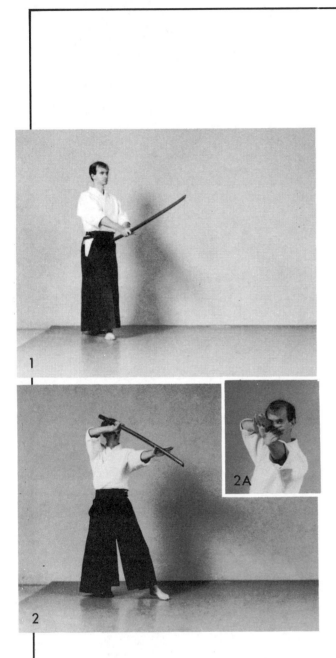

Tori-i (Upward Block) and Shomen Uchi

Like kiriage, the method of tori-i is one which has direct roots in the combative strategy of the feudal age swordsman. Tori-i means a "flicking bird's tail" and the name refers to the rapid motion of the blade as it moves upward at the side of the body, and then cuts down again, much as a long-tailed bird bobs that appendage as it flits from branch to branch. To make tori-i, (1) begin in a right chudan kamae. (2) Step forward, letting go the sword handle with your left hand and turning the bokken slightly, with the blade pointing to the right as you move. Continue the motion, rotating the bokken and bringing it up until the blade is directed straight

up and the length of the weapon is at the level of your ear. As you lift the bokken, (2A) reach out with the left hand and catch the weapon's ridge in the space between thumb and forefinger. Slide it along that part of the hand until it is in position. (3) Step forward again, this time with the left foot, raising the bokken up and turning it over, to (4&5) strike down in shomen uchi. Like kiriage, tori-i should be thought of as both a parry and a cut upward. It is a good example of the maxim of *koboichi* (attack and block are one). Do not practice tori-i solely as a block and counter, nor as two attacks, but as a combination of both.

Nihogiri
(Cutting in Two Directions)
—First Form

Nihogiri is a fundamental exercise designed to improve shifting. There are two

methods of training in it. For the first, (1) assume chudan kamae. (2-6) Step forward,

3

4

5

Continued

6

7

making shomen uchi. (7-9) Pivoting on the balls of both feet, turn 180 degrees to the right, facing the opposite direction and raising the bokken to jodan. (10) Step forward again with the left leg and strike again with shomen uchi.

Nihogiri—Second Form

The second form of nihogiri calls for a single step, then a pivot, and a slide, in the manner of tsugi ashi. (1) Begin in chudan. (2&3) Step forward with the lead (right) foot, cutting in shomen uchi. (4&5) Pivot to your left, turning 180 degrees, and (6-8) cut again in shomen uchi. During the second strike, draw the left leg back to assume a natural sankakudai stance. The feeling in this combination should be as if one were being attacked by an enemy in front and behind. Step in and cut the first, in front of you, then turn and, drawing yourself back to avoid the second attacker's blow, cut him at the same time.

Shihogiri
(Cutting in Four Directions)

Nihogiri should eventually be expanded, enabling the student to cut in four directions, or shihogiri. This exercise requires even more attention to balance and posture, and if it is regularly engaged in with devotion and spirit, it will be the foundation for excellent technique. To make shihogiri, (1) begin in right chudan kamae. (2-5) Step forward with the right foot, executing shomen uchi. (6-9) Turn and cut in the reverse

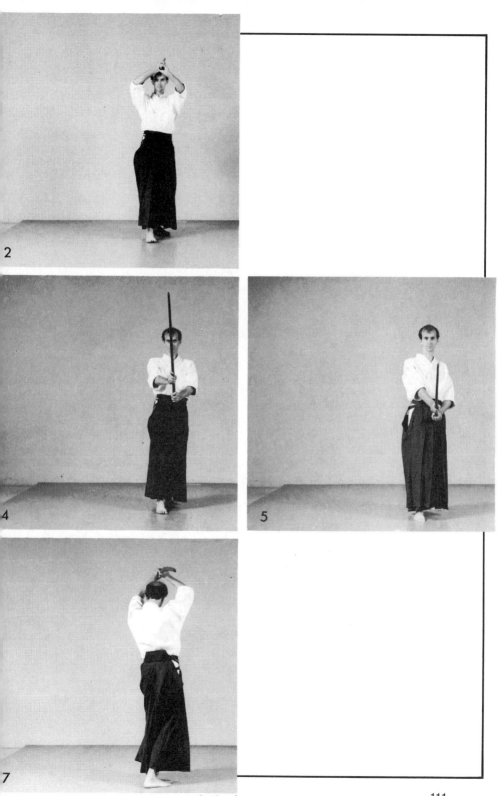

2

4

5

7

Continued

direction, as with nihogiri. (10-14) Pivot on the balls of both feet 270 degrees to the right, (15-17) stepping forward with the right foot, cutting with shomen uchi

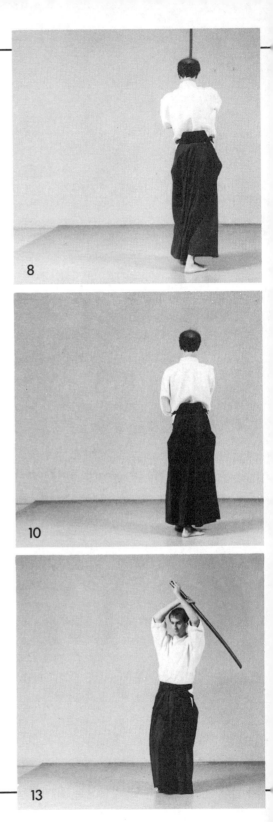

11

12

14

15

Continued

16

again. (18-21) Turn back to the left, without reversing the stance, and (22&23) cut down once more. Shihogiri should be practiced quite slowly at first, making certain each technique is fully focused and all movements are correct. Gradually, begin to make the strikes flow with one another, until there is a contrast motion, with no space left for an attacker to move in. The spirit of shihogiri is one of being assailed by a number of opponents, and moving against them, dodging their blows and connecting with one's own.

18

21

Shihogiri—Another Angle

(1) From right chudan kamae, (2) step forward with the right foot, and (3) execute shomen uchi. (4) Pivot 180 degrees to the left on the balls of both feet, and (5&6) cut down as with nihogiri, sliding the left foot back toward you as you strike. Your next strike will be to your left, but you will come to face that direction by turning 270 degrees to your right. (7) Pivot to your right on the balls of both

2

4

5

7

Continued

feet. (8) As you cross the 180-degree point, continue turning another 90 degrees by shifting your right foot around to point in that direction, stepping forward with your right foot, and (9&10) cutting with shomen uchi. (11) Pivot on the balls of both feet to your left 180 degrees, and (12-15) cut down once more.

Nihogiri from Iaigoshi

Nihogiri may also be performed from the sitting position of iaigoshi. Sadly neglected among swordsmen today, cutting practice from iaigoshi is one of the best ways of developing the body

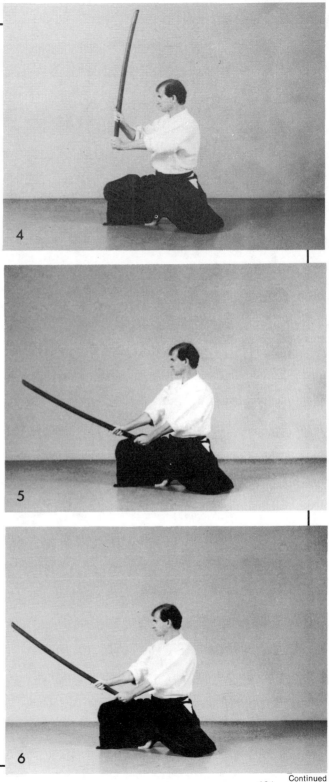

properly. (1) From iaigoshi with the right leg leading, slide the right foot forward, (2&3) bring the body up behind it, and raise the bokken into jodan. (4-6) Cut down in shomen uchi. These move-

Continued

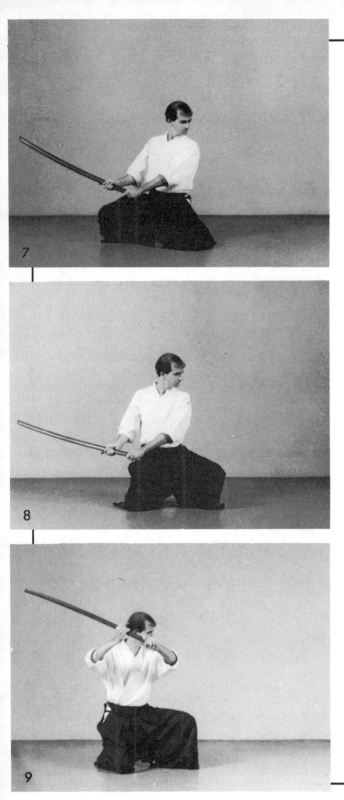

ments should all be performed as one action. (7-9) Pivot 180 degrees on the balls of both feet to the left, (10-12) cutting in the opposite direction as the body settles. It is important to coordinate the strike with the

forward slide of the feet and body, and the second strike with the settling of the body's center of balance after the pivot. Do not lift the hips at all during any of these movements.

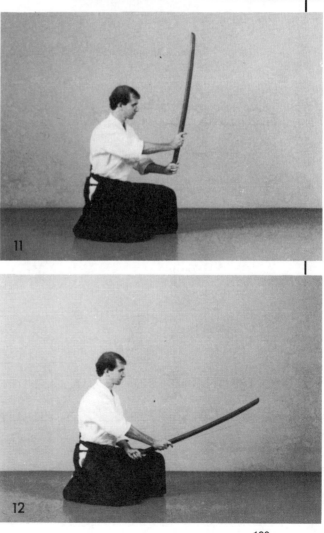

Naname Giri from Iaigoshi

Of course, it is possible to practice any other of the basic strikes from iaigoshi. As an example, naname giri from iaigoshi. (1) Beginning in iaigoshi with the right leg leading, (2&3) slide forward (4&5) cutting down at the diagonal angle

1

3

2

4

5

125 Continued

of naname giri. (6) Pivot, (7-11) bringing the bokken around to strike at the opposite angle to your rear. Since the bokken must strike at opposing angles and be raised as the practitioner pivots, care must be taken to maintain proper balance and positioning.

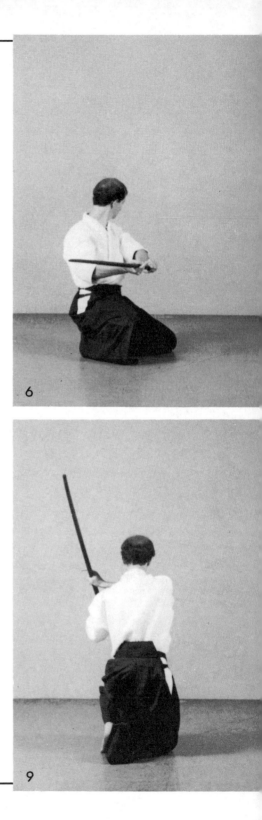

6

9

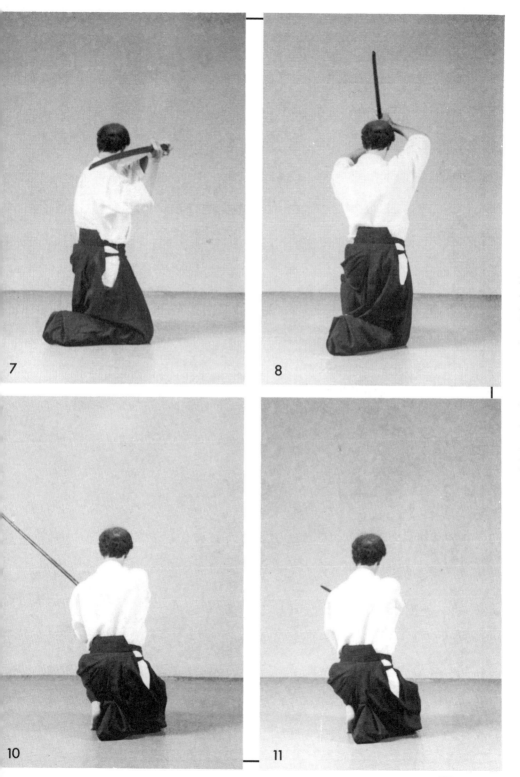

7

8

10

11

Naname Giri and
Yoko Uchi Stepping Forward

(1) Starting in chudan position, (2&3) slide your lead foot forward as you raise the bokken to jodan, then (4-6) strike down in naname giri as your step is

1

3

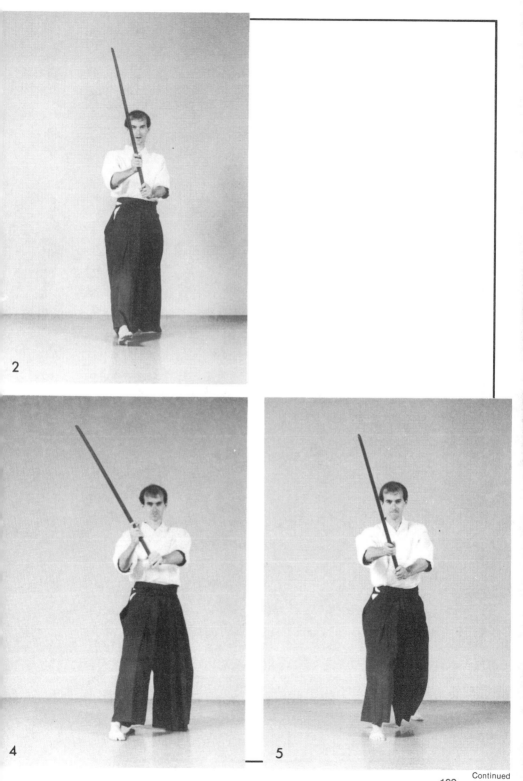

2

4

5

129 Continued

completed. (7&8) Slide forward with the other foot, raising the bokken again to jodan, and (9&10) tilting the bokken to the other side, strike with yoko uchi as the step is completed.

6

8

10

Shomen Uchi Stepping Forward and Yoko Uchi with Two Steps Forward

(1) Starting in chudan position, (2&3) step directly forward, raising the bokken into jodan, and (4-6) strike down with

2

3

5

6

Continued

shomen uchi as your step is completed. (7&8) Step forward again as you raise the bokken into jodan, and (9&10) step forward once more, (11) tilting the bokken into position. Then (12&13) cut with yoko uchi as your final step is completed. Such combinations require a change in timing between the bokken and the lower body and serve to sharpen your basic skills.

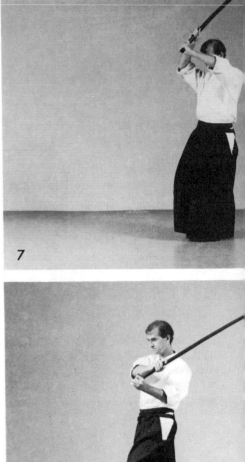

7

10

11

Shomen Uchi Taking
Two Steps Back
Then Two Steps Forward

(1) Start in chudan with your right leg forward. (2-4) Step back with your right leg, raising the bokken into jodan. The bokken comes up to jodan with the *completion* of this first step back, not before. With the bokken in jodan, (5-7) take a

2

4

5

7

Continued

second step back, and (8) cut down with shomen uchi as this second step is completed. (9-11) Now, step forward, raising the bokken up to jodan with the completion of the step forward, then (12&13) take another step forward with the bokken in jodan, and (14) cut down with shomen uchi as this second step forward is completed.

Combination Exercise

To close this discussion of combination techniques, here is one exercise which is a good one for building strength and flexibility in the wrists, as well as for coordination. These two areas are often a problem for beginners in suburi training. (1) Begin with the bokken in the right hasso kamae. (2&3) Stepping forward in sankakudai, drop the tip of the bokken by relaxing both wrists. (4) Describe a large arc in front of yourself as you continue to step forward and (5) as you complete the step, raise the bokken up into a

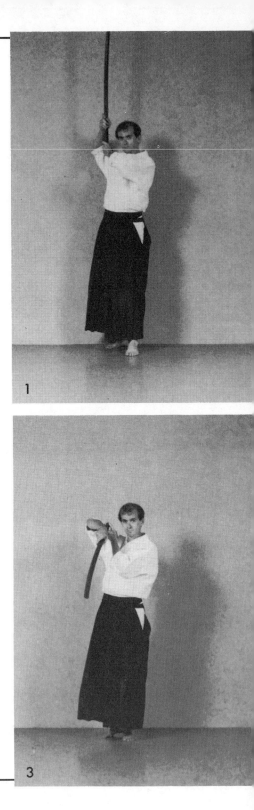

2

4

5

Continued

141

left hasso kamae. (6) From the left hasso kamae position, repeat the same movements. (7&8) Drop the point of the bokken by relaxing your wrists, and as you (9&10) step forward with your left foot, continue to swing the bokken through a circular path in front of your

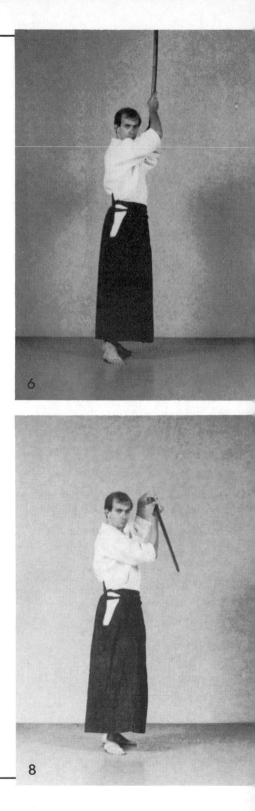

6

8

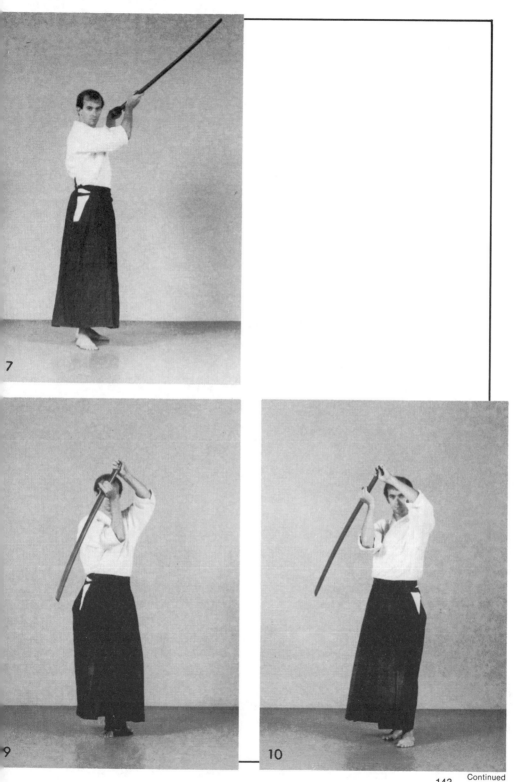

7

9

10

143 Continued

11

body to come back to (11&12) a right hasso kamae position. Then again (13) drop the point of the bokken, (14) swing it across the front of your body as you step forward with your right foot, and (15&16) bring the bokken up to establish a left hasso kamae position. Try to make the bokken stop at the same instant the step is completed and force the wrists to do the work of moving it, never raising or lowering the elbows. This is also a fine exercise for use with the heavier suburito.

14

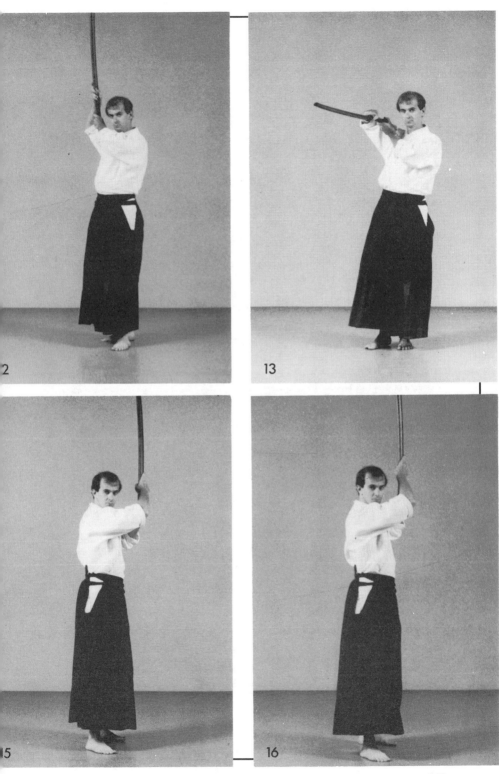

Why do you fix your eyes on the
swinging sword? His grip reveals where
he wants to cut.
—Morihei Uyeshiba, of Hombu aikido

KUMITACHI
(Techniques with a Partner)

Kumitachi is a term used in suburi training which means "swords coming together." It connotes those exercises with the bokken that are performed with a partner. There is an understandable tendency to look upon kumitachi as a form of contest or as a kind of prearranged duel, with a designated winner and loser. Such ideas, though, are utterly antithetical to the practice of kumitachi. Instead, the point of these partner exercises is to practice basic techniques and to employ skills of distancing and timing against a real opponent. If kumitachi is engaged in with a spirit of competition, the stronger or more advanced practitioner will, it is true, humiliate and confound his partner, and so in that sense, he may be considered to have "won." But in a far more important way, he will have lost entirely and the practice session will have been a complete waste of time for him and his partner. Kumitachi should be entered into with a feeling of blending your movements with that of your partner, and of moving in harmony. In this regard, the concepts of winner and loser are superfluous.

This, however, should not be misinterpreted. There is all the difference in the world between softness and weakness. If kumitachi is allowed to degenerate into a balletic *pas de deux,* without focus or effort, its intent is equally perverted. Partners should work together, using their strength to help one another polish and perfect technique. When making a strike in kumitachi, approach it as if it were one that would actually kill the opponent with a single blow. If this spirit is maintained, no matter how soft or hard the exchange itself, the meaning of kumitachi will have been accomplished.

Since it is expected that you will not even attempt to engage in kumitachi until you are completely familiar with the basic strikes and movements of solo suburi training, there is no need to go into detail in the instructions for kumitachi's specific sequences. Instead you should use the illustrations as a primary guide.

A

Ma-ai
(Combative Distancing)

Preparatory to engaging in kumitachi practice, the practitioners need to be aware of *ma-ai* (combative distancing). In suburi, three kinds of ma-ai are recognized. (A) The first is *itto issoku ma-ai.* Here, the partners are separated by about a third of a meter. One step forward by either will bring them both into striking range. This is implied by the name itself—itto issoku means "one sword; one step." This one step ma-ai is the customary distance used in most kumitachi. (B) The second ma-ai variation is that of *toi ma-ai,* wherein the *kissaki* (tips) of the bokken just touch. This was a dangerous but favorite distancing for a famous swordsman of old Japan, who explained it as the secret of his success in dueling. Coming close enough to touch the point of his opponent's weapon, he could feel whether it was being held stiffly, or with a calm suppleness. If the grip was of the former kind, he was sure of his victory. If it was the latter, though, it indicated a very skilled warrior, and in that case he would quickly flee the scene. (C) The last ma-ai is that of *chikama ma-ai*, with the top third of the bokken crossing the opponent's. It is at this distance that the outcome of the encounter, should it be a real battle, will already have been decided. For kumitachi practice, begin exclusively in the itto issoku ma-ai, as it will impart a good sense of distancing, rhythm, and timing.

B

C

First Kumitachi

(1) Both you, and your partner, begin in right chudan kamae. (2) Your partner steps in, making shomen uchi, while you (3-5) step to your left front corner in naname okuri ashi to avoid

the blow. When escaping your partner's attack, it is important to control it as well. You must time your counterstrike to smother the attack from above, (5A) cutting down against his

bokken at such an angle that the attack is nullified and controlled. Contact must be made at a point along the blade where the curvature of the bokken is deepest. (6&7) Pivoting toward your right, slide your bokken along your partner's, maintaining control. (8) Continue your rotation, (9) stepping back as it is completed, to (10) strike with shomen uchi.

Second Kumitachi

(1) Both you and your partner begin in right chudan kamae. (2&3) As your partner advances with his right foot, making shomen uchi, (4) move forward, pivoting. And then, (5) stepping back to your left front corner to avoid his cut, (6&7) strike at the same time in shomen uchi. Timing on your part is understandably crucial. You must step deeply into your partner's attack and cut down decisively as you turn.

Third Kumitachi

(1) Both you and your partner face each other in right chudan kamae. (2&3) Stepping at an angle to your respective right front corners, both stike with shomen uchi. As your partner (4) raises the bokken to strike again, (5&6) shift straight

forward to direct a thrust to his throat. You must time your second attack to catch him in the jodan position. If your thrust is too soon, it can be parried; if it is too late, you will be struck by his second attack.

Fourth Kumitachi

This is a variation of the third kumitachi. One purpose of this kumitachi is to train you to forestall an attack until you can shift into a more advantageous position. (1) Both begin in right chudan kamae. As your partner raises his bokken to strike with shomen uchi, sliding in with his right foot, you also slide forward with your right foot, (2&3) pre-

empting the blow by aiming your thrust against your partner's throat. You must direct the point of your bokken in such a way and with such firm spirit that your partner's strike is halted. You then (4&5) shift to your left side, allowing your partner to complete his strike, at the same time (6) you step back to cut down with shomen uchi.

Fifth Kumitachi

(1) Starting in right chudan kamae, both you and your partner (2) step with your right feet to your respective right front corners in naname okuri ashi, lifting the bokken in the circular movement on the left in preparation for yoko uchi. (3) Arc the

bokken to the right side, and (4) strike down with yoko uchi. (5) Yoko uchi here is aimed a bit lower than as it is practiced in basic suburi. Both of you make your strikes at the level of the opponent's upper thigh. (6) Begin to withdraw your bok-

ken. (7) Both of you step to your respective left front corners, circling the bokken up on the right side, (8) arcing it overhead, and (9) down

on the left side (10) to strike once more with yoko uchi. (11&12) Your partner steps forward with his right foot,

Continued

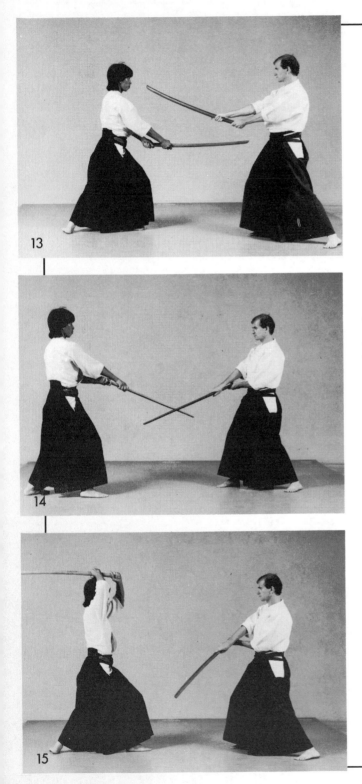

raising his bokken into jodan. You also raise your
bokken into jodan. (13) As
your partner strikes down
with shomen uchi, you shift
slightly to your left, avoiding
his strike, and cutting down
with shomen uchi. (14) Both
of you pause momentarily.
Then, your partner crosses
his bokken under yours. (15)
He deflects your bokken
aside in the same motion
with which he raises his own

bokken into jodan. You allow him to deflect your bokken, and use this momentum to swing your bokken over to the left side. (16) Slide back as your partner strikes down with shomen uchi, and use the force of his parry to circle your bokken up on the left side (17) into jodan. As your partner completes his cut, shift forward and (18) cut down in your own shomen uchi.

Sixth Kumitachi

(1) You and your partner both begin in right chudan kamae. (2-5) Both of you step forward and to your respective lefts in naname okuri ashi, striking simultaneously with yoko uchi. (6&7) Your partner advances with the lead (right) leg, striking with shomen uchi while you shift back to your left rear corner to avoid the blow. As he completes his strike, (8) slide in and cut down with shomen uchi.

Seventh Kumitachi

(1) Both you and your partner begin in right chudan kamae. (2-4) Both of you strike with naname giri,

stepping with the right leg. (5) Sliding to your respective lefts, both of you reverse this movement, (6&7) strik-

169 Continued

ing with naname giri to the opposite side of the body. As your partner (8&9) raises his bokken to cut forward

with shomen uchi, (10) lower your sword and (11&12) step in deeply, cutting into and up against his midsection.

Eighth Kumitachi

(1) Both you and your partner assume chudan kamae with the right foot forward. (2&3) Both of you begin by sliding forward and lifting the bokken into jodan, to (4&5) strike simultaneously with naname giri. As your partner (6) takes another step directly to his front, preparing to cut with shomen uchi, (7) step

2

4

5

7

Continued

back to your left corner, (8) raising your bokken, and (9) as he cuts down, (10) parry his strike with tori-i. (11) Bring your bokken overhead. (12) Shifting your weight forward, (13) begin to bring the bokken down, guiding it with your left hand by the ridge of the blade as you step forward to your right front corner. (14) Cut down against your partner's forearms as you complete the step. (15) Guide the bokken with your left hand as you cut down on his forearms. (15A) Be sure your left hand rests safely along the ridge of the blade, guiding it and helping to apply force to the cutting action.

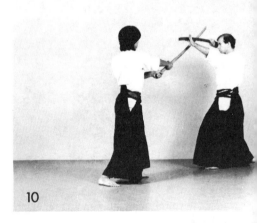

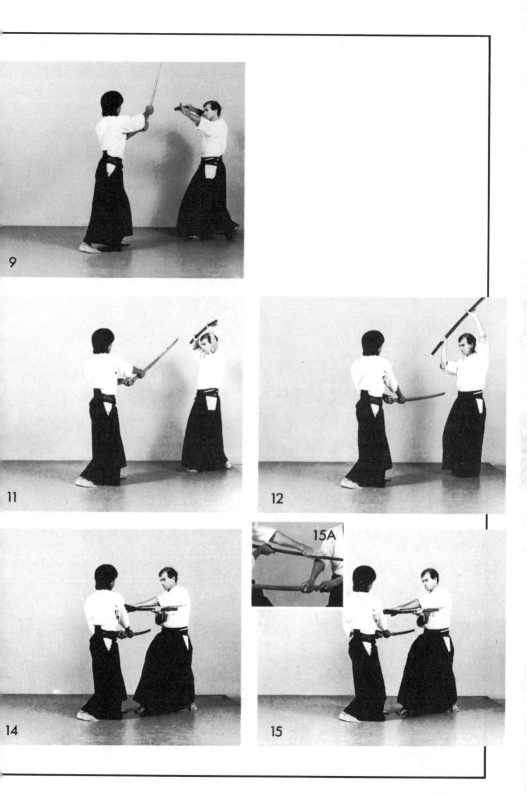

Ninth Kumitachi

(1) Both you and your partner begin in right chudan kamae. (2) Both of you begin raising your bokken (3) into jodan as you slide forward. (4&5) Both of you strike with naname giri. As your partner

(6) slides his lead foot back, raising his bokken into jodan for another strike, lower your bokken slightly, and move your left foot slightly to the left in preparation for a left rearward shift

Continued

away from his strike. As he (7&8) begins to step forward with his left foot, begin to shift to your left rear corner, protecting yourself with the upward motion of kiriage. (9) Shift completely out of the way, raising your bokken with kiriage as your partner steps forward with his left

foot, and cuts down with shomen uchi. (10) As he raises his bokken into jodan once more stepping forward with his right, step in with your left foot from his left side, and (11) cut down with shomen uchi, (12) focusing the strike at his head.

Tenth Kumitachi

(1) Both you and your partner begin in right chudan kamae. (2) Both of you slide your lead foot forward as you begin to raise your bok-

ken to strike with yoko uchi. (3) Bring the bokken up and (4) into jodan. Then (5) as you both complete your forward

6

7

8

step, (6) strike with yoko uchi. Before your partner would withdraw his bokken, (7) step slightly to your right front corner to attain an advantage in leverage. (8) Step forward, continuing the momentum of the initial strike. (9) Press your partner's bokken back. Because of your slight shift to your right front corner, as you (10) press directly forward, your partner's resistance is di-

rected at an angle off the side of his line of force, enabling you to shear in off his right side while (11) your bokken cuts across his midsection. If you depend upon your strength alone to break his balance and form, you will be unsuccessful and the exercise will be nothing but a pushing match. You must shift your body to the correct angle to break his defense.

Do not think that this is all there is.
More and more magnificent teachings
exist—the Way of the Sword is
unfathomable. The world is wide, full of
occurrences. Keep that in mind and
never believe "I am the only one who
knows."
　　　　　—Yamaoka Tesshu, of Muto-ryu

ZAREI
(The Seated Bow)

There's no better way to close this explanation of training in the art of the Japanese sword than to provide a description of the proper method of making the seated bow *(zarei)*. Since ancient times, the ability to bow correctly in Japan has been a sign of manners and breeding, and it remains so today in the various classically inspired arts of that country. The budoka who begins and ends his training sessions with bows to the dojo, to the memory of the masters who've gone before, and to his partner, accomplishes more than just a manifestation of courtesy and respect. He also demonstrates a sense of purpose and self-worth that are the best evidence of his having elevated the art of killing with the sword into a way of living with it.

Assuming the Seated Position
for Zarei

To make zarei, (1) begin in a normal standing position, the heels touching. Without bending at the waist, (2) drop down onto the left knee. (3-5) Turn the bokken over, using the left hand, so the hilt is pointed to the front, at the same time lowering the right leg to stand on both knees. (6) Keeping the upper body straight, sit back slowly, resting the buttocks on the tops of the heels, with both insteps placed flat on the floor, and place the bokken on the left side.

1

4

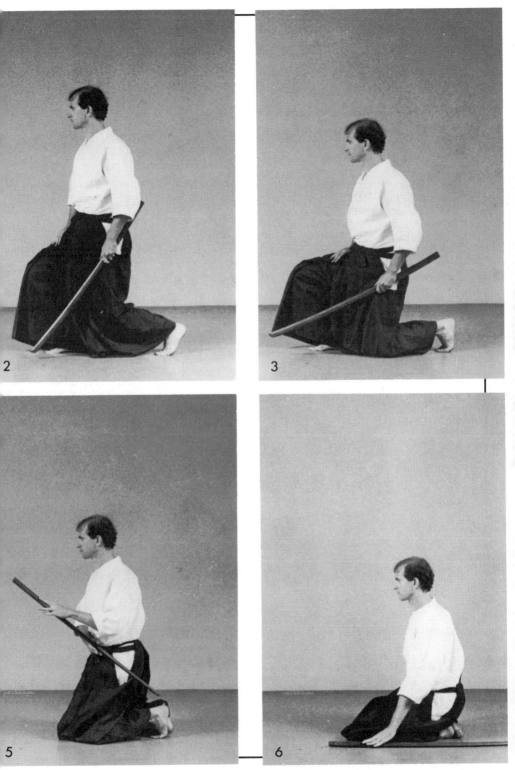

2

3

5

6

Bowing in Zarei

(1) With both palms resting on the upper thighs, keep the chin tucked in and the ears on a vertical line with the shoulders. (2) Reach forward with the left hand, placing it flat on the floor, fingers angled to the right. (3) Place the right palm beside it, then (4) lower the upper trunk in a bow. It is important to keep the gaze directed about a meter to one's front. Do not look straight down or bend the head at the neck. After completing the bow, (5-7) reverse the procedure until you are once again in a sitting position.

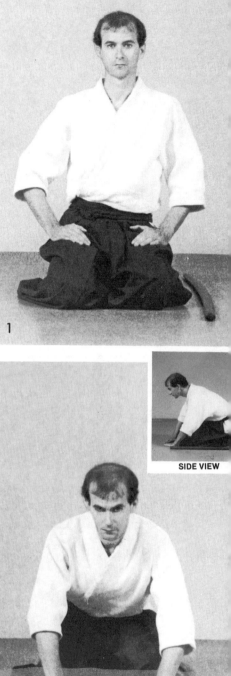

1

SIDE VIEW

SIDE VIEW

4

5

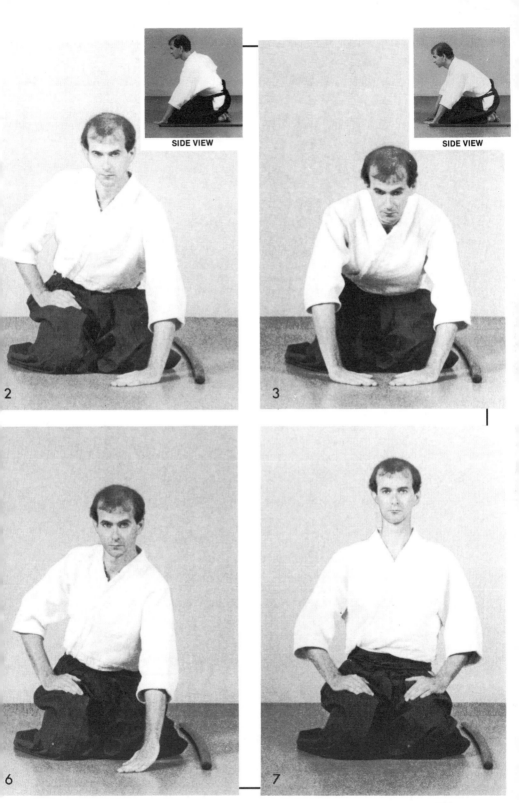

Glossary

Bokken—The wooden practice sword used as a substitute for a steel blade in suburi practice. The bokken matches in weight and shape the approximate dimensions of a real sword. Depending upon its exact size or construction, the bokken may also be called *bokuto, kaisuburito, suburito, hakusuburito,* or *Jigen suburito.*

Bokuto—Another term for the bokken.

Chudan—Middle level.

Do—A path or Way. In Japanese, do refers to any of several disciplines designed to train the practitioner in technical skills which have as their ultimate goal, the perfection of the spirit.

Gedan—Lower level.

Giri—A suffix meaning to cut. When used as a prefix or by itself, giri is pronounced *"kiri."*

Gyaku—Reverse.

Hakama—The pleated, split skirt worn by practitioners of several martial arts and Ways. Also known as a *joba hakama.*

Hasso—A position of combat with the sword held vertically and the hands level or slightly above the shoulders.

Hidari—Left direction.

Iaigoshi—A form of crouching which enables rapid movement and balance in any direction.

Jodan—Upper level.

Kamae—A posture which reflects combative spirit.

Kata—A form, or a series of formalized movements, used for training in the martial arts and Ways.

Katana—The steel sword of Japan, customarily worn with the cutting edge up, thrust through a sash at the hip. When the sword is attached to the sash with a connecting cord and worn with the cutting edge down, it is called a *tachi*. The katana may also be referred to as a *shinken* (real blade) to distinguish it from the bokken.

Ken—A blade or sword. Ken is used as a prefix in several words relating to swordsmanship, including *kenjutsu* (sword art), *kendo* (sword Way), *kenshi* (swordsman), etc.

Kiri—To cut. When used as a suffix, this word is pronounced *"giri,"* e.g., naname giri.

Kiriage—To cut or slash upward.

Kumitachi—A short, two man exercise with the sword or bokken. Kumitachi is not a contest, but a form of practice between partners.

Ma-ai—The various forms of distancing between opponents or partners training together.

Migi—Right direction.

Naname—Diagonal or oblique.

Nihogiri—Cutting *(giri)* in two *(ni)* directions *(ho)*.

Obi—A sash or belt.

Renraku—A combination.

Riai—The interrelationship of principles. Riai refers to the similarities in body movement, distancing, and timing involved in meeting an opponent, whether one is armed or empty handed. In a larger sense, riai also refers to the similarities in principles and goals of all the Japanese Ways.

Ryu—The school or tradition of a specific martial art.

Sankakudai—The basic stance taken in suburi training, with the front foot pointing forward and the rear out at slightly less than a 90-degree angle, forming a triangle.

Shihogiri—Cutting *(giri)* in four *(shi)* directions *(ho)*.

Shikko—A method of walking on the knees and balls of the feet while crouched in the iaigoshi position.

Shinai—The mock weapon used in kendo. The shinai is made of split lengths of bamboo tied together. It is lighter than a real sword, has no curvature, and is manipulated in an entirely different way than the steel sword or bokken.

Shinken—The live or sharpened steel sword.

Shomen—The front.

Suburi—Methods of swinging and striking with the bokken.

Suburito—Another name for the bokken.

Tachi—Another term for the Japanese sword.

Tai sabaki—Body movement.

Tori-i—A method of striking or blocking upward with the sword, using one hand to support the blade. Literally, tori-i refers to the rapid movement of a bird's tail, which this action resembles.

Tsugi ashi—A sliding step, advancing the feet while maintaining contact with the floor in a light, shuffling motion.

Tsuki—To thrust.

Uchi—To strike.

Uwagi—The heavy cotton jacket worn while training.

Waki—The side or lateral. *Waki gamae* refers to a position with the sword held out and back at the swordsman's side.

Waza—A technique.

Yoko—Another term to denote the side. A lateral strike to the midsection of the body is called *yoko uchi*.

Zarei—A formal sitting bow.

Zubon—Pants or trousers, worn during suburi training underneath the hakama.

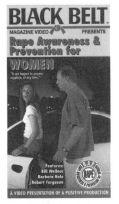

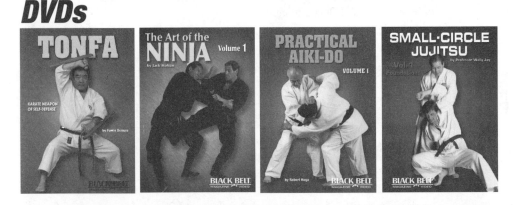